PRAISE FOR

community
of
KINDNESS

Steve Sjogren and Rob Lewin cheerfully debunk myths surrounding church planting, as they fire off one marvelously irritating concept after another to get us scratching our heads and our hearts about starting new churches. This is a fabulous collage of spiritual/mental snapshots taken over the years and stored in the memory banks of one of today's most respected church leaders (Steve). Opening it at any page is like chatting with your own church-planting coach, whose advice and stories make your experiences with starting a new church seem normative—and still hopeful. This is a must-read for all church planters and their teams.

DANIEL A. BROWN, PH.D.
SENIOR PASTOR, THE COASTLANDS FOURSQUARE CHURCH
APTOS, CALIFORNIA

Start reading this book anywhere—and the energetic, provocative style will jump-start your creative juices. Here is a book full of practical, no-nonsense—and often counterintuitive—wisdom on topic after topic related to the planting and nurturing of a church. I scribbled in the margins as I read, but I realized that all al[ong the] way God was making His own marks on my heart and m[ind.] I'm recommending this book to anyone who wants to [see] Christ's kingdom grow.

DR. STEVE HAYNER
PASTOR AND FORMER PRESIDENT, INTERVARSITY
CHRISTIAN FELLOWSHIP

Though my approach to church planting has evolved into something significantly different from the one outlined in this book, I have long witnessed, respected, admired and sought to emulate the "otherliness" that overflows from the pages of this book—especially for the poor, the least, the last and the lost. A church plant of any style will be guided toward the heart of God to the degree they follow Steve and Rob there.

TODD HUNTER
DIRECTOR, ALLELON FOUNDATION
FORMER NATIONAL DIRECTOR, VINEYARD-USA

Wisdom says that if you want to know how to do something, first listen to those who've been there and done it. Steve Sjogren and Rob Lewin are two seasoned veterans that have been there and are still doing it. And you'd be wise to listen to what they have to say in their wisdom-laced book *Community of Kindness*.

DR. AUBREY MALPHURS
PRESIDENT, VISION MINISTRIES INTERNATIONAL
PROFESSOR, DALLAS THEOLOGICAL SEMINARY

All great communicators have one thing in common: They know how to connect. Through servant evangelism, Steve Sjogren has connected with the people of Cincinnati and beyond, and in the process planted and built one of America's great churches. He is a living example of how it can be done. Through the pages of this book, Steve and his coauthor Rob Lewin will connect with all new and future church planters. But sharing 106 great challenges, Sjogren and Lewin offer something for anyone who is launching or wants to start a church.

JOHN C. MAXWELL
FOUNDER, THE INJOY GROUP

There are heroes among us: intrepid, creative, dedicated men and women with the calling and courage to plant new churches. They deserve our respect and support, and they deserve a great resource like *Community of Kindness*. It's an honest, wise, balanced voice of experience that will spare you learning a lot of things "the hard way," because the authors already have.

BRIAN MCLAREN
PASTOR (CRCC.ORG)
AUTHOR AND SENIOR FELLOW IN EMERGENT (EMERGENTVILLAGE.ORG)

Church planting is certainly hard work, but it should not suck the life from those doing the work, Steve Sjogren and Rob Lewin understand that and provide this material as a contribution to the worldwide effort of church planting as a life-giving experience for all involved.

DOUG PAGITT
PASTOR, SOLOMON'S PORCH
MINNEAPOLIS, MINNESOTA

I love it! This is required reading for every church planter. Everything you need to think about is in this book. I highly recommend it to every church planter and it will be a mainstay with all of the interns and church planters in our church.

BOB ROBERTS
NORTHWOOD CHURCH
KELLER, TEXAS

The coaching of Steve Sjogren and Rob Lewin has been invaluable to me as a church planter and to the eternal harvest of souls. I pray that every church will learn as I have learned from them. A must-read!

DOUG ROE
SENIOR PASTOR, VINEYARD CHURCH
DAYTON, OHIO

Community of Kindness gives the reader an opportunity to receive counsel and insight from seasoned and effective church planters. This book is crammed full of practical wisdom and useful advice. There are valuable lessons on every page.

CHUCK SMITH, JR.
AUTHOR, *THE END OF THE WORLD AS WE KNOW IT* AND *EPIPHANY* (SOON TO BE RELEASED)

Steve Sjogren and Rob Lewin are wrong about one thing. They say only 1 in 100 pastors is capable of starting a new congregation. But that's before this book. Here is that rare resource that dramatically increases possibilities—and dreams.

LEONARD SWEET
DREW THEOLOGICAL SCHOOL, GEORGE FOX UNIVERSITY
PREACHINGPLUS.COM

community *of* KINDNESS

STEVE SJOGREN & ROB LEWIN

Regal

From Gospel Light
Ventura, California, U.S.A.

PUBLISHED BY REGAL BOOKS
FROM GOSPEL LIGHT
VENTURA, CALIFORNIA, U.S.A.
Regal PRINTED IN THE U.S.A.

Regal Books is a ministry of Gospel Light, a Christian publisher dedicated to serving the local church. We believe God's vision for Gospel Light is to provide church leaders with biblical, user-friendly materials that will help them evangelize, disciple and minister to children, youth and families.

It is our prayer that this Regal book will help you discover biblical truth for your own life and help you meet the needs of others. May God richly bless you.

For a free catalog of resources from Regal Books/Gospel Light, please call your Christian supplier or contact us at 1-800-4-GOSPEL *or* www.regalbooks.com.

All Scripture quotations are taken from the *King James Version*. Authorized King James Version.

Cover and interior design by Robert Williams
Edited by Steven Lawson

Library of Congress Cataloging-in-Publication Data
Sjogren, Steve, 1955-
  Community of kindness / Steve Sjogren and Rob Lewin.
    p. cm.
  ISBN 0-8307-2972-0
  1. Church development, New. I. Lewin, Rob. II. Title.
  BV652.24 .S58 2003
  254'.1–dc21   2002152004

3 4 5 6 7 8 9 10 11 12 13 14 15 16 17 18 / 12 11 10 09 08 07 06 05

Rights for publishing this book in other languages are contracted by Gospel Light Worldwide, the international nonprofit ministry of Gospel Light. Gospel Light Worldwide also provides publishing and technical assistance to international publishers dedicated to producing Sunday School and Vacation Bible School curricula and books in the languages of the world. For additional information, visit www.gospellightworldwide.org; write to Gospel Light Worldwide, P.O. Box 3875, Ventura, CA 93006; or send an e-mail to info@gospellightworldwide.org.

DEDICATIONS

STEVE SJOGREN

To Rebekah and Laura—thanks for putting up with all
of our church-planting adventures over the years.
You've been real sports! I love you.

ROB LEWIN

To Lilly—the greatest person I've ever known.

CONTENTS

ou can do anything else, do it. You're in charge of pennies, not dol
n new church will have a unique way to do the tasks of ministry. Pec
re on; deal with it. Recognize that a very large percentage of the f
ch you gather will be already-converted people. What do you dro
ut? Is it a big church—or changed people? Lame facilities are OK.
. A lousy attitude isn't. Staff turnover is normal, not a sign of lurl
. Begin to delegate now. Have fun on the journey. Don't be pi

LET'S DIALOGUE

This book has been written for postmodern church planters who seek to reach mainstream America. Our intent is to challenge, not to tell you what to do.

We want to build a dialogue. To help you better interact with our ideas and experiences, we have broken the book into levels and points. We have divided this book into levels because it is better understood when seen moving from one point of depth in the planting process to the next. We have more than 100 points along the way to telling our stories and to make it a snappy and memorable read—and quite frankly both of us have ADD (attention deficit disorder)! We think in bursts, so that is the way we have written this book. We hope you don't have to have ADD as well to make sense of it all.

The title *Community of Kindness* is very similar to my (Steve's) book *Conspiracy of Kindness* that came out a few years ago (anniversary edition, Servant Books, 2003). *Conspiracy's* message is all about going out to reach people who are not-yet Christians in creative ways. That is an incredibly important message that the Church needs to grab onto. *Community of Kindness* answers the questions, What do you do once people have come to check out the church? and How do you create an environment that is loving, accepting, full of grace and forgiveness? In other words, this second book deals with what you do with people once they come to the party after they've been invited through servant evangelism.

Some of the points you will find relevant, others irrelevant. We actually hope you will differ with some of them. It would be boring if everyone agreed with all that we have written. Certainly no one will concur with all 106 points. Take the meat and leave the bones.

You will notice that there are a lot of references to the concept of servant evangelism in these pages. Servant evangelism, which I (Steve) wrote about in *Conspiracy of Kindness*, is a way of sharing the good news of Christ with others in your community through simple, practical means that can be done by people in everyday situations—from washing cars to giving away soft drinks to cleaning up a neighbor's yard. Each of these is done for free to show the love of Christ in a practical way. Every small act of love and kindness piles upon another to make a big impression and eventually to define your church and its vision to the city in powerful ways.

The subtitle of this book could easily be *Church Planting Through Servant Evangelism*. We believe that servant evangelism is simply the most effective means for gathering a crowd in the process of church planting. It is a tremendous tool in getting your people into the community to begin to change the spiritual climate. It is a versatile and profound instrument to use in the planting process.

We are more than happy to assist you with your adventures in church planting. We'd be happy to connect with you by e-mail to discuss these things further—church planters are our favorite people on the planet! Here are our personal e-mail addresses and my (Steve's) servant-evangelism website—a very helpful resource for anyone getting started in servant-evangelism outreach. The website contains several hundred servant-evangelism outreach projects and lots of success stories of others who have used it in their church plants. Also, at the website you can purchase outreach tools and training resources galore.

rlewin@fuse.net
sjogren@cincyvineyard.com
www.servantevangelism.com

SO, YOU WANT TO PLANT A CHURCH

Today's Church is in tremendous need of excellent congrega-tions. And excellent local churches are led by excellent pastors. You are an unusual person if you can plant a church. There are probably one in a hundred pastors who are capable of launching a new congregation.

This book is all about encouraging and instructing pastors who aspire to this sort of ministry calling.

The landscape of America's church scene is bleak from the perspective of church health. Jack Dennison, in his excellent book *City Reaching*, suggests that we need to start approximately 300,000 churches—right now.[1] So, yes, you are an unusual per-son if you can plant a church, but we need to see God raise up a large army of people just like you. You are the hope of the American Church scene. Without thousands—make that tens of thousands—of new and vibrant churches springing up all over the country in our generation, we are in big trouble.

A study was conducted at Fuller Theological Seminary regarding the innate gift orientation of a large study group of pastors.[2] The research concluded that 85 percent of pastors are wired to maintain local churches in the day-to-day running of ministry. These kinds of leaders enjoy running the church for the long run. Another 10 percent are "organizing" pastors who enjoy administrating the actions of the church. These sorts of pastors flourish in the wake of a fast-paced congregation that is on the move in their community. They can make order out of seeming chaos. Finally, the smallest grouping, just 5 percent, came out as catalytic—that is, they were able to cause things to happen out of seemingly nothing. These were people who made positive explosions erupt all around them on a regular basis. They didn't blow things up in a chaotic, disorderly way necessarily, but they caused progress to happen in places where life had gotten bogged down. Most church planters fall into a subset of this catalytic group. Being generous, perhaps 1 percent of pastors are capable of planting a church and not losing their sanity.

This book is unique in that the writers themselves have planted a number of churches directly and have coached indirectly dozens of other churches into existence.

There are a lot of potential church planters disheartened these days with the advent of many books on the topic of postmodernism. For many, the more they read on the topic, the less sure they are that they can possibly plant an effective church in the changing climate of our culture. Additionally, if a church plant is even possible, they become convinced that it will be a very expensive venture.

We take the opposite viewpoint. We've read many books on postmodernism and think that we have come to understand the topic as well as most pastors. Sure, there are new and challenging issues facing us today, and indeed, the culture is moving away from whatever trappings of outward Christian framework that existed just a few decades ago; but the place our culture finds itself in does not and cannot change the mission of the Church. We have been called to reach out radically to a lost and dying world that is without hope apart from Jesus Christ. If all our reading on postmodernism causes us to think differently, we need to challenge the authors. We have planted lots of churches with very few resources. As I (Steve) write, I am coaching a half dozen churches into existence with the average plant receiving around $10,000 in start-up support. Based on our track record, most of these plants will succeed and even thrive to become sizeable churches.

ASSUMPTIONS FOR READING THIS BOOK

- We contradict ourselves on purpose. What? Yes we do. This church-planting enterprise has lots of facets. Any planter will need to be able to deal with two opposing thoughts at the same time and hold each as true. This thinking is something we will revisit many times in the course of this book.
- Our lists are random for a reason. We intentionally allowed the different topics to mingle with others that seemingly have nothing to do with each other. And they don't, except that they are all important. So please don't be frustrated. View the book as Forrest Gump would, like a box of chocolates: "You never know what you're gonna get!"
- We believe that your church is important; your church is the hope for America.

- We believe that you can be successful—however you define that.
- We believe that the skills of being a great pastor are learnable—by you. We believe that God is on your side—He is into your dream, big or small.
- Church planting hurts. Scott Peck wrote, "The definition of mental illness is the avoidance of pain."[3] We have friends who disagree, but most often our experience is that planting reveals to the planter and team members many of the personal weaknesses they would prefer not to see.
- A slightly balanced life is possible. If you demand complete balance like what your friends with regular jobs enjoy, then you will fail.
- It's good to laugh at yourself. In this book, we will laugh at ourselves.
- We believe that a church that doesn't do outreach is a waste of time.
- We believe that anything that keeps you from being effective for Jesus is negative.
- We believe there is nothing sacred in this process except the forward progress of the kingdom of God.
- We believe that one of the foremost qualities that makes for church-planting success is great humility of heart.
- We believe that serving the poor and disenfranchised is mission number one at every level.
- We believe the power of God's love is what brings people to Christ—not slick programs, not telling people how bad they are, not evangelism and not theology.
- We believe that God loves your city more than you do. He has been caring about that geography since people first arrived.

- We aren't committed to any particular flavor of ministry. We believe that almost any flavor can work in a church plant.
- We believe that the simple approach of serving people in practical ways in the community is the most effective means of connecting your new church with the city where God has placed you. This book is filled with references to the value of servant evangelism. I've had many people ask me how to include servant evangelism in church planting. The short answer: Just do it!

Notes

1. Jack Dennison, *City Reaching* (Pasadena, CA: William Carey Library, 1999), pp. 39, 41. Dennison states that of the 375,000 churches in America 70 to 80 percent are dysfunctional.
2. Carl George and J. V. Thomas, *Multiplying Churches: Planting New Congregations In and Nearby Existing Ones,* Extended Training Modules and Planning Resources, vol. 5 (Diamond Bar, CA: Center for the Development of Leadership for Ministry, n.d.), n.p.
3. Scott Peck, *The Road Less Traveled* (New York: Touch Stone Books, 1978), p. 17.

ou can do anything else, do it. You're in charge of pennies, not doll
n new church will have a unique way to do the tasks of ministry. Pe
re on; deal with it. Recognize that a very large percentage of the
h you gather will be already-converted people. What do you dre
ut? Is it a big church—or changed people? Lame facilities are OK
. A lousy attitude isn't. Staff turnover is normal, not a sign of lur
Begin to delegate now. Have fun on the journey. Don't be pl

MISSION

1 | What do you dream about? Is it a big church—or changed people?

It's not a large enough dream simply to focus your hope on a big church. There are plenty of big churches that are ineffective. Statistically, larger churches are less effective at discipling and evangelizing than medium-sized churches.

One of my (Steve's) favorite passages in literature is from Annie Dillard. She captures well the ideas of meaning, risk management and living life in balance.

> There is always the temptation in life to diddle around making itsy-bitsy friends and meals and journeys for years on end. It is all so self-conscious, so apparently moral. . . . I won't have it. The world is wilder than that in all directions, more dangerous . . . more extravagant and bright. We are making hay when we should be making whoopee; we are raising tomatoes when we should be raising Cain, or Lazarus.[1]

This is where your view of discipleship makes an enormous difference. The question is how can we build disciples who will be world changers? Assuming that a classroom-only church will make action-based disciples or hoping that some politician will fix the problems the world faces is lunacy. Neither of these has ever helped. Only individuals empowered by the Holy Spirit will meet the needs of suffering people.

When you discipline yourself to count only changed lives and new believers launched into the world to be with people in real ways and enabled to live big lives that count for eternity, then you won't be misled by money growth, attendance growth, important people in attendance or media coverage.

2 | Decide where you want to fit on the missional continuum—become either a come-and-see or a go-and-do church.

A come-and-see church prioritizes its resources (time, energy, money, etc.) toward the building, attendance and membership. Often people in come-and-see churches vie for named positions of esteem. To acquire the positions, they may even lobby others, similar to what happens in a political campaign. When this happens, leaders spend time on issues relating to members, not outsiders.

Surprisingly most of these churches espouse believing in outreach, releasing the laity, caring for the poor and giving generously. Deep down somewhere, doesn't everybody? After all, you can't be much of a Bible reader and not know how important these issues were to Jesus Himself. But there is a serious difference between knowing that these are important issues and making them primary in how you communicate with a disciple. The come-and-see church *says* these things are important but then doesn't make them priorities.

How can you know which kind of church you are? A good test is to ask what percentage of your annual budget is spent on serving the poor. What percentage is spent on making sure disciples are with people "in the world," loving and serving them in their current lost condition with no strings attached? That's right, no strings. What percentage of the volunteer hours at your church are spent on lost, needy, unconverted folks who can't add to the church in any way? Do volunteers stuff bulletins, teach classes, ask others in the church for money or serve on committees? These are still important matters, after all.

The go-and-do church empowers volunteers to serve not-yet-converted people.

The go-and-do church turns that view of church life upside-down—actually inverting those ideas; that is, empowering volunteers to serve not-yet-converted people. The objective of the go-and-do church mentality is to make sure that lots of money is spent on those who cannot pay you back. And it says to be vigilant in leadership against the natural gravity of letting the church serve itself.

1. The go-and-do church allocates 10 to 20 percent of its annual income to serve the poor! *What? Are you nuts?* Yes, perhaps we are!

2. The go-and-do church makes sure that 50 percent of all the volunteer hours at the church are invested in folks who don't even care about the church, aren't Christians and need to be shown love in practical ways.

OK, guys. Really? How?

We recommend that you take time with your leaders and explain this to them. They need to get this. One idea: Start giving 5 percent to the poor. *Now.* It will change your life, all your people and especially your leaders. Then add an additional .5 percent each quarter till you get to 10 percent. That process will take almost three years.

Wow! Well, guys, that's great, but we already give 10 percent of our income to the denomination, and now we're supposed to give away another 10 percent? How? Where do we get it?

We understand. This change of the financial policy of a congregation is pure lightning. It also becomes intentionally missional. It's worth every discussion it provokes and every person who instantly becomes your enemy for no good reason except, "I don't want my money spent on them!" It's a marker, a separator and a change agent. It serves as a great barometer of current attitudes. The feedback you get will be a valuable insight into your people's hearts.

- Value "do" over "know." Analyze your conversations each week based on this criterion: Which of the people I spoke to were exited about going and doing? Maybe they had an idea. Maybe they already tried something. Maybe they were coming back after trying some ministry in some way and had news they wanted to share with you. *Note: All of these people are doers. Spend your time with them! Focus your energy on the people who are already doing something, not the people who are waiting for you to do something.*
- Know the location where spiritual experience happens, or recognize the church as a force, where believers are sent to do spiritual things outside of church.
- Old Testament worshipers of God had a come-and-

see arrangement. God was confined to being in one place at a time in His dealings with people. He was in the holy of holies in the Temple, or He manifested Himself in the burning bush before Moses. As the story of the Bible unfolds, it becomes increasingly a go-and-do book. When we get to the second chapter of Acts, the presence of God is no longer confined to one person (Jesus) or one place, but He is released upon the Church. From that point forward He becomes a God who is invading the world through His released people who are moving forward as a force upon the face of Earth.

• Right from the beginning determine to be a go-and-do church rather than a come-and-see one. The go-and-do church powerfully expresses the missional heart of God for the world. Both God and people are looking for go-and-do churches to join themselves to. These are exciting churches where the Spirit of God is continually on the move. These are the churches worth joining.

One of the major obstacles in Christendom today is the existence of come-and-see churches. There are too many observers and too few activists.

Once an inward-focused perspective has developed, it's difficult to turn a church from come-and-see to go-and-do later in its existence. Steer your new church in an outward direction right from the start, when it is small and pliable. No matter what price you pay to build this sort of church, it will yield tremendous results.

• Servant evangelism builds a go-and-do community of believers.

Show Love

On Fridays we (Steve's church) conduct what we call Community Blitzes where we go into the city with 6 to 10 different simultaneous outreaches. We do a little bit of every sort of servant evangelism, from a soft drink giveaway at a busy intersection to a free car wash to dorm-room cleaning at the local university. Our goal is to touch as many people as possible with God's love in the course of two to three hours. With soft drinks alone, we have extended our-selves to as many as 6,000 people in half an hour.

It's all a matter of organ-ization and expectation. When several dozen people are involved in pulling off an outreach such as this—a blitz around the community— there is a tremendous amount of excitement. It's downright

3 | Find your own way.

You must respect and honor everyone's tradition. God has brought the gospel to you through the hands of others and by their hard work. But if honoring them requires you to ignore the current call-ing of Christ in your life, you must choose the way of Christ. For some this may come at great cost.

If you wait for permission from your sponsoring group, you will never get far very quickly or efficiently. Don't spend time worrying about your actions too much. *Is what I'm doing really the denom-ination's style?* That sort of concern will handcuff you and keep you from church-planting effectiveness.

Some churches can be described as high Episcopal while others could be called high Vineyard, according to their tradition—that is, they are conforming to the most rigorous traditions of the group with which they are affiliated. They are more concerned with those tra-ditions than they are with their total effectiveness in the community. We believe that "high" anything equals a nongrowing church virtually all of the time. No offense is intended toward any group. But those who put the primacy of paying homage to their group will not have adequate energy to pour themselves into the task of properly planting a thriving church.

4 | Make belonging synonymous with doing.

This is not about works, but identification. Too often being part of a group has to do with affirming a set of doctrines or values. It's only natural—it's the way the system of church in America has been established. Usually membership in a group is connected with belief, not with actions.

You must communicate that the aim of your church is to produce disciples who do stuff, not disciples who only know stuff.

Servant evangelism is all about activating people into ministry. There are no observers. Everyone is a participant in the spiritual army, and serving others shows that they are part of the whole.

The atmosphere you create is what leaks out of your life when you aren't looking. If you are going to have "belonging" and "doing" as one and the same, you must communicate that all the time. That communication is a 24/7 matter that comes across in all that you as a leader do and everything for which you stand. It is something that you live out passionately

contagious. The greatest value to doing servant evangelism in various contexts is that church planters look much bigger than they are with just a few people. In some blitzes, we've gotten other churches involved as well. Our numbers have swollen greatly. We have expanded the number of outreaches to over a dozen options at many locations around town. We have touched as many as 15,000 people in just a few hours. More important than the number of people being touched by the outreaches is the expansion of the perspective of those doing the outreaches. We are seeing many Christians doing outreach who had previously been stuck in a come-and-see church lifestyle. That's worth getting excited about.

so that your people see it firsthand at work in and through your life. There are lots of leaders who say they want people to serve the poor and do outreach, but to be effective you must carry out

Servant evangelism is all about activating people into ministry. There are no observers.

those activities as a matter of course week in and week out. These are very attractive ingredients that will be a primary attractor to your fellowship as the city comes to check you out. This flavor will affect all that goes on in your fellowship from the initial entry point of newcomers. We have noticed that people decide within the first two minutes whether or not they like a church.

We are also including integrity. At some point we have to do what we believe in. At the Vineyard Community Church in Cincinnati, you're not really "us" if you haven't raked a yard full of leaves or delivered a bag of groceries. When it came time to go out to care for the needy, I (Steve) didn't ask if others wanted to do it or not; I simply said, "Here we go! Would you like to drive or be a passenger?" When we went to clean toilets I would ask, "Would you rather wash the porcelain or the windows?" It's not a matter of *if* but *how* and *when*.

What are the actions that you and your team believe make up a true disciple? What transforming actions do you want them to do? Lives need to be transformed, not just information passed along. We need to go beyond transformation into building people who do something that fundamentally changes the way the world operates.

Some ideas:

- Take Thanksgiving dinner to a family who would not have gotten a dinner otherwise.
- Instead of making your Christmas gathering an "us only" event, make it inclusive, creating one where your people go out into the community with the love of Christ and apply it in practical ways.

5 | Are you cut out to plant a church?

Who has the makeup to plant a church? A person who

- has passion to see others experience the love of God.
- can't find a place of ministry elsewhere.
- has a history of helping people experience the love of God.
- has some experience in a church plant.
- has a big heart for expanding the kingdom of God.
- is capable of living on less than they've earned.
- has counted the cost by talking with someone who has successfully planted a church.

Show Love

For the past several years at Vineyard Community Church in Cincinnati, we (Steve's church) have been shortening our Christmas Eve services in favor of going out to do servant-evangelism projects. We gather to sing traditional songs and to light candles, and then we adjourn to go out into the highways and byways with donuts. We go out to those who have to work on Christmas Eve and would rather be at home than working on that night. We offer them the good donuts and prayer and a Christmas carol. We go to police and fire stations and restaurants. Most of my favorite stories have come along as I drive through fast-food restaurants and surprise the managers by giving food rather than asking for food on that most special of nights.

- has a spouse who is excited about planting a church.
- has a history of being able to gather people to new ventures.
- is known by others who have planted churches and can recommend you without reservation.

Who isn't molded to plant a church? A person

- who does it out of the wrong motivation.
- who doesn't want to work hard.
- who is expecting it to be less work than it will be.
- who doesn't expect to be emotionally and spiritually torn up by God.
- who doesn't have any other opportunities in life.
- who wants to reproduce religious environments (we don't need any more of those).
- who wants a desk job.
- who wants to live life at a slow pace.
- who wants to be everybody's dad.
- who wants to proclaim to the world that "I've made it" in a venture.

The truth is that you aren't going to attach your personal worth to whether your church plant makes it or not.

6 | Consider the primary traits of an excellent church planter.

The opposite is true. You are starting this because the church is about the city, the people of the city—it's about them.

I'm not sure how well I (Steve) would have scored on an assessment if I had taken it at certain points of my life.

In the end you will have to go with what God has put in your heart.

Listen to God. Listen to your spouse. Listen to your advisers and coaches.

In the end you will have to go with what God has put in your heart.

Look at your history. It's always true that the best indicator of future behavior is past performance. I have always been in charge of things. I have always sold things. I have always led groups.

It's difficult to say that there is a typical church planter. The best training for church planting is to be a staff member of a successful plant. The next best training is to be on the staff of a church that successfully reaches the lost. The third best training is to have failed one or two times as a senior leader.

Diligence knows how to keep on keeping on.

It's the ability to improvise. It doesn't insist on having perfect conditions for work to occur.

It's the skill of being able to grow a vision into a reality.

The ideal profile of a church planter:

- Former insurance salesman
- Grew up on a farm
- Entrepreneur

Former Insurance Salesman

If you've been in sales, you know that what you work for is an intangible. You wake up unemployed every day. Nothing happens until someone buys something from you each day (apply that to the church world). You're only successful if you are a self-starter; you're only successful if you can communicate vision, gain a future result and dream for a better life. A man is attached to his family and the responsibility he has to his family. If you can't communicate the adventure of this thrill of a new life, then you might as well forget about it because you will not be able to succeed. Communicate this in the positive.

Grew Up on a Farm

You have the ability to innovate—that is, you have the "MacGyver skill." You have the ability to fix complicated things with a minimum of resources and time constraints. You are able to live sanely with chaos that is outside of your control. Crops, bugs and weather issues don't scare you off.

Entrepreneur

With a church plant you're creating something that has never existed before. You are getting people to think differently than they've ever thought before. You're putting together an entire business. From top to bottom, you are assembling it: marketing, merchandising, public relations, disasters, organization, development, hiring and firing and finances.

You feel comfortable hanging out in an environment where outward thinking and high momentum is a way of life. Perhaps you're already doing all the stuff that you would do to plant a church while still on the staff of an established church. There's a key formula that you must have: taking responsibility for both the dollars and the results. Then you will learn valuable lessons.

Working hard anywhere as a routine is a vital discipline. Getting used to that behavior is always good.

One last thought: You might be surprised by how many Christian luminaries failed multiple times at planting a church before they succeeded. For example, Jack Hayford was fresh off of a failure with a church plant in Indiana when he came to Van Nuys, California, to pastor what became known as The Church On The Way. He was tempted to give up but told the Lord he would give it one more try. If you've read any of his books or have attended his church, aren't you glad he gave it one more try?

7 | Minimize your list of conditions and requirements before stepping out to plant.

What is a true impediment to planting a church?

The first thing you have to erase from the page of obstacles is money. Some people think you almost have to be independently wealthy before you can plant a church. The truth: Normal people do it all the time. If you've been exposed to some good models, have a chosen city, have some experience and have a dream, then there's no reason to not start meeting with a group of people. The truth: You can simply start a Bible study at your house. At first, no one has to know that you have it in mind to start a church. At the appropriate time, though, you will need to let your leaders know.

Here, however, is a set of issues that you need to take into consideration because they are true impediments to beginning a church plant. Do not pursue church planting if these issues are present in your life.

- If you don't think your marriage can handle it, it probably won't.
- If you are deep in debt, it creates an environment of desperation. You need the group to grow to pay for your salary just to be able to pay your debt. We assume

most people have debt, but that is manageable debt. It can't be so large that it spiritually and emotionally affects the decisions you make as a church leader.

- If you know you are involved in outright moral sin, it is not a good idea to get involved in starting a church.
- If you have difficult sexual issues, don't plant a church. Most people have some sexual issues in their lives. What we are talking about is what is clearly beyond the norm.
- If there is a question about your own mental health— you are honestly concerned about your mental health— it's probably not a good idea to plant at this time.

On the other hand, you don't have to be formally theologically trained. Some of the largest churches in the U.S. are led by nontheologically-trained people. You don't have to be perfect and you don't have to live a pain-free life. God is seeking available people.

Notes
1. Annie Dillard, *Pilgrim at Tinker Creek* (New York: HarperCollins, 1990), p. 258.

ou can do anything else, do it. You're in charge of pennies, not doll
n new church will have a unique way to do the tasks of ministry. Pea
e on; deal with it. Recognize that a very large percentage of the f
ch you gather will be already-converted people. What do you dro
ut? Is it a big church—or changed people? Lame facilities are OK.
. A lousy attitude isn't. Staff turnover is normal, not a sign of lurl
. Begin to delegate now. Have fun on the journey. Don't be pl

PERSONNEL

8

Discern the "scaffolding people" you will attract at the first phase of your plant from the "permanent building" people who will rise up later.

In every church plant, there are two kinds of people—*many* are there for just a season, and *a few* are there to stay long-term. This is a vital lesson to learn, because as a leader it is easy to become caught up in the nurturing of what we lovingly call the "scaffolding people." Builders of physical structures use a set of scaffolding to erect a building. The scaffolding is not the building, but it is necessary for the construction of the building that will eventually emerge. As the building nears completion, the scaffolding falls away, leaving the permanent building standing. In the same way, there is human scaffolding that will help you erect a new church. While they aren't part of the permanent building, they are vital to leaders in the building of the permanent congregation that is to come.

Scaffolding people are wonderful folks. They are part of the flock of God. He loves them and, we suspect, so do you; but it simply doesn't make good sense to pour unlimited amounts of energy into these ships that are passing in the night.

All of the churches we have started and coached have begun with a sizeable percentage of scaffolding people. These individuals are drawn to new churches. Some of them are pretty normal, but because of the places in life where they find themselves, they are not able to make a significant commitment to your church, or perhaps even to God.

Sometimes scaffolding people are peculiar. They tend to be drawn to new churches because often they lack a stable social network in their personal lives. Many of them have been rejected by people in their old networks due to a lack of social skills.

Are scaffolding people valuable to a church plant? Absolutely! In fact, they are vital. Scaffolding people aren't just warm bodies that will fill empty seats—they are a big-time gift from God! They are there temporarily but will still contribute to your forward progress. They give of their finances. They are able to make small commitments to serve (we don't recommend you put a person you suspect is going to be a temporary plant in a place of key leadership—resist the temptation and listen to your intuition).

How do you recognize scaffolding people? Most often they are already Christians. You'll find that those you lead to Christ, or those who connect to Jesus because of your community, are real leaders and are permanent parts of the life of God among you.

Often scaffolding folks are in the midst of early- to mid-career timetables, destining them to be relocated by their companies. Many are hurting, oddball types who are looking for unconditional love and acceptance—people who are carrying around lots of emotional baggage. Peter calls Christians a "peculiar people" (1 Pet. 2:9), but some are more peculiar than others! Just realize that in Phase 1 (your first couple of years) you will be a scaffolding magnet, attracting disenfranchised people in your town—including many from other churches. As Norm in *Cheers* would say, "Not to worry!" Good will come of this. Just don't let them absorb too much of your focus and time.

These people will leave your church, sooner rather than later. Most of those leaving, according to exit interviews, will report that there is a lack of connection with the pastor. In other words, they most commonly leave because they don't like you. But

Many people come and go on your way toward attaining critical mass.

don't let that worry you. Especially in the first few years you will have many people coming and going on your way toward attaining critical mass.

Don't take it personally. It's just a part of life.

9 | **Recognize that a very large percentage of the first batch you gather will be already-converted people.**

Everyone wants to grow with conversion expansion from the get-go, but that's not the way it works.

Already-converted people sometimes have peculiar ways of seeing things. Their viewpoints can get in the way of the progress of your new church. When they get tired or frustrated, they'll leave for greener pastures. The people you win, or who find Christ among you, stay forever if they can. They buy in, serve, give, pray, sweep the floors and take care of the babies

Get Smart

when no one else will. This is almost universal. It's the family of God version of "blood is thicker than water." As you serve, care and reach out, take them with you. Model for them the reality that being a believer has to do with action and that action is directed at somebody else. Require them to bring their friends and let them do it, too! Why? Because the already-saved will sometimes want to argue about almost anything and talk about action, wasting the time you could use to serve and to love your city to Christ! Leave them alone. Let them go on and on about their theology, views, opinions, books they've read and conferences they've attended. You, on the other hand, go out with the people who will follow you and love somebody!

Attracting already-saved believers is just the way it is in Phase 1 in a church plant. We have found that evangelism happens in Phase 2 and later.

The already-converted are attracted to a flavor. When they discover you're not their flavor, they may well leave. Many will be with you for a season, but when they figure out what you are really about, they will be gone. It's disappointing, but that's life. You must remain philosophical about it all. For many, the most you can do for them is love them and equip them for life and ministry while they are with you, and bless them when they leave.

Desperation makes us hungry for results. There's nothing wrong with a cry for practical results that will work.

During Phase 1 of your plant, you will be gathering already-believing people in by the batches. These will be people who are looking for an alternative to the already-existing church world.

Don't be dismayed and think, *A lot of good I'm doing. I'm just providing another alternative to the church menu.* Not so! You need a base of the already-converted to build upon. Hopefully they are flexible and open to new ideas and new ways of doing things.

relevant, inviting place. Our already-gathered people began to gather their not-yet-Christian friends to celebrations, and we began to grow in significant ways. So, did servant evangelism grow our church? Yes, in two ways. Initially, it caused us to begin to look beyond ourselves. Later, those we touched in the community began to come as a result of being loved in the name of Jesus.

Phase 2 comes after you have gathered the first 200 people. When you've achieved synergy with the community around you, the people begin to self-gather.

10 | Don't be picky. You're looking for warm bodies!

You can't be picky for the first few years of your church's existence. Your attitude has to be, *We'll enthusiastically take* anyone *here!*

One Monday after church, I (Steve) was just wasted emotionally and physically. For some reason this Monday was a particularly difficult one for me. I couldn't get past remembering all the hurting people I had encountered over the weekend. I made

Show Love

a declaration to my wife, Janie: "That's it—I've had enough of this church-planting thing. I quit! And I mean it this time." Janie has heard this kind of talk many times in the past, so she was unimpressed by my expressions of frustration. We talked for a while about my feelings, and she then suggested I take a drive and pray through some of my feelings. As I was walking out the door she called out, "By the way, can you pick me up a burrito at Taco Bell on your way back?"

I drove around for an hour or so praying prayers of ventilation to the Lord. On my way back home, I remembered my wife's request and pulled into the drive-through lane of Taco Bell. As I waited for the order to come up in the long line, I felt the Lord speak to my heart. I sensed Him saying, "Open the door to your car and I will give you a gift." At first I thought that couldn't possibly be right. After all, what sort of gift could the Lord give me in the parking lot of Taco Bell? But curiosity got the best of me and I opened the door. There on the asphalt was what looked like a blackened piece of chewing gum. As I looked more carefully it turned out to be a penny that had been run over so many times that tire tread had turned it black. I first thought, *Great, Lord. You've given me a discarded penny as a gift. Thanks a lot.* I took a key and pried it up from the ground. With a glob of asphalt still clinging to it, I held it in my hand and simply began to weep. I realized that God *had* given me a gift—one of gathering discarded pennies. I sensed the Lord speaking to me once again. "For the rest of your life I am going to give you discarded pennies to watch over. If you will be diligent in watching over them, you will have plenty of wealth to accumulate. Lots of pennies add up."

In servant evangelism we are constantly collecting discarded pennies. One of our favorite pennies is a guy named Carl. He comes out of a 12-step recovery background. Over a period of years people from our church had served him a number of times in various servant-evangelism projects. He reports that we had washed his car, given him a soft drink, wrapped a Christmas present for him and cleaned the toilets at the pizza place where he works. After all of these acts of generosity, his curiosity got the best of him, and one day he came to church. He said he was touched by the atmosphere he encountered. After listening to the

> **The kinds of people who are looking to join a church plant are the lost, the least and the lonely.**

messages for several months he slowly found his way to Christ and was baptized. He is now one of our most avid servant evangelists. He is very consistent in going out on Saturdays to show God's love in practical ways. He is a team leader for servant-evangelism outreaches.

The kinds of people who are looking to join a church plant are the lost, the least and the lonely. If you are looking for just the pretty and together people, you are likely missing the majority of people that God wants to send your direction. It's all about finding the most significant people in the discarded parts—in the parts that have been determined to be of no worth in other church systems.

There are also many churched people who are looking for a place where they can plug in their ministry gifts. Many are frustrated in other churches because they are untapped resources who are not being used.

In church-growth circles there is a lot of talk about planting churches that are made up of homogenous groups. The conclusion is that growing churches are made up of groups of people who are like one another. On the other hand, we have never sought to attract groups that were like one another, yet we have grown to a large size. Because servant evangelism has been the primary drawing card of my (Steve's) church plants, we have always drawn a great cross section of the city. Servant evangelism touches everybody in the city. When you invite the city to come to church, the city tends to show up. That's natural diversity.

It wasn't my intention to build a diverse group when I started. The fact is that when you serve, you don't—you can't—choose the type of people who come. Those who show up define the makeup of the group.

11 | Staff turnover is normal, not a sign of lurking evil.

Resist the exhausting notion that all your time, effort and training are wasted. Probably someone else is now training *your* next staff person!

Isn't that a great way to look at the matter of staff transitions?

Let's look at the hiring practices of the esteemed Procter and Gamble company. They have a worldwide reputation as a great trainer of brand managers. When headhunters and companies such as Dial, Clorox and Dow "shop" for brand managers, they look at current Procter and Gamble employees because they are the best-trained people in the industry. In Cincinnati it is said that when you are chosen for a position at Procter and Gamble, you are the best in the industry. Everyone knows that Procter and Gamble hires the best, and that working there means you will work for, be trained by and partner with the best managers in the industry. Procter and Gamble management encourages employees who decide to leave to tell their bosses as soon as possible. That way they don't have people representing them who don't want to be there and may be bitter. They have great outplacement services. So they treat you like a winner when you leave, too. This gives them time to find a replacement and train them. This all allows the person leaving to have a positive experience. After all, they may be dealing with the company from a different position soon. Isn't that a great model? The employee is never demeaned, never chastised. Procter and Gamble only wants those people who want to be there. And when you don't want to be there any longer, they treat you with respect.

What is to be learned here?

1. Not everyone stays forever.
2. Even when you hire the best, many leave.
3. Departures can be done in a respectful, peaceful way.
4. When people leave, it creates a place for new winners to prove themselves.

What if you take our advice, yet things still don't go well and you are left with an angry exit interview? An angry exit interview is a wonderful teacher. Why? Because you can identify why the person doesn't want to be with you—this is worthwhile. The question is whether or not you are adult enough to hear their legitimate complaints, even if they are hostile.

12 | Avoid the Jesus-Judas complex.

In the course of church planting you will often find yourself desperate for talented personnel. Every so often someone will come along who seems larger than life (a Jesus type). This person seems as though he or she can do no wrong and has no limits to his or her gifting. He or she seems like a direct and profound answer to prayer. Best of all, you will be able to put your leadership on cruise control. Upon his or her arrival, it's easy to begin to think, *This person will be the answer to all my ministry problems. I will be able to off-load all of my weighty problems and extra responsibilities onto this proven individual. Hurrah!*

Make minimal commitments to new people no matter how gifted they are.

What typically happens is that within 24 months that relationship will have degenerated to the point where this person transforms into a Judas type and leaves the organization as a scapegoat. The reality is that this person probably was not as talented as you perceived him or her to be. You were simply desperate for talent. It simply takes time in any organization for relationships to settle in and reality about people's actual skill levels to become apparent.

Newcomers to the staff environment deserve the opportunity to get to know you and your church from the ground up. For everybody's safety, make minimal commitments to new people no matter how gifted they are. That way no one will get hurt.

One tool to avoid the Jesus-Judas complex has been employed by Pastor Jack Hayford in Van Nuys, California. Often Pastor Jack would hire gifted leaders from other churches. Rather than allowing them to move directly into pastoral ministry, they were required to serve as the janitor for the church for up to a year. Jack knew the intrinsic lesson: People only follow servants. This tool had the added benefit of removing the Jesus expectation almost completely. It also allowed leaders up to a year to find out if this was really a good place for them. They could decide that it wasn't without creating significant trauma in ongoing ministries. While you may not be able to make your number-two person the janitor, using Pastor Jack's process as a guide for reducing the speed at which new people have authority can be extremely helpful. Finally, it's a tremendous character check and a way to see the humility and the spirituality of the people you've hired. Do they chafe at having no visibility? Do they grumble at not being able to preach? Do they whine that this work has no value? Then they clearly aren't the people who you want to have visibility.

13 | Realize that most of the first 200 people you gather will leave within two years.

When we consult with new church-planting teams, there is often a moment at the beginning of the plant when an exciting meeting has taken place. Potential leaders have shown up and made verbal commitments. You look at their enthusiastic faces and promises of commitment. They all seem like they are on board for life! But then life happens and people leave—including the ones who seem the most committed.

As we sit in the living room of the enthusiastic pastor of this church plant, the conversation comes around to the future. We hate to burst his or her bubble, but we have to speak the truth. "You know something, although this is exciting, two years from now all but two or three of these people will be gone. That's just the way that it works."

How depressing! Why does this happen?

People have unrealistic expectations about what your church will be like, what you will be like, what your relationship with them will be like. They don't know you or your style. They don't know your dream yet. When they run into the full force of your dream, they may decide it's not their dream. Church planters need to master the skill of living between two worlds. On one hand, you know before you start that there is a revolving door, and on the other hand, you care deeply about the spiritual life of your city. If

Some of our best volunteers and leaders were on the way out the door when they saw a need.

you have a proper balance, when someone says, "You've changed" or "I thought this was going to be a different kind of church, but it's the same as every other church," you will be prepared.

They may like your teaching—at first—but receiving it as weekly fare may become too much. I have heard many people say they didn't like the worship of the new, smaller church when they have come from a larger, established congregation. Knowing this information will help you deal with the situation more effectively on an emotional level, and you will be less likely to get entangled in the situation, but it will not spare you the pain that you will face.

How do you maintain your self-esteem on the one hand and let people leave freely on the other?

Let's set the situation. It's after your morning service and Joan has waited to speak with you. So, you begin to dialogue. She proceeds, "We've just decided to leave. We don't like the children's ministry."

We've heard that hundreds of times.

Here is a time-tested approach for finishing this conversation with peace and confidence:

Tell me about what you were thinking or looking for.

The information you are going to get in response is vital. Their comments also occasionally reveal that "the thing" they first mentioned isn't really "the thing," and they can't actually articulate why they are leaving. They may say they want all the things you don't want. That's great! It means you have accurately communicated who you are. On the other hand, they may tell you the worst about your church. Listen and learn a lot. Invite them to be a part of the solution if they have a valid criticism that needs attention. Some of our best volunteers and leaders were on the way out the door when they saw a need and had ideas about how to better the situation. We challenged them, and they stayed to become part of the solution.

I have a list of churches that are like that to which I can direct you.

Tell them right to their face, "People are free to make their own decisions here." They may just stay, because they are so excited that you really do what you say you do—that is, you treat them like adults.

Also, in offering them a list of other churches in town you are making it clear that you aren't the only show around and that you actually know what other churches are doing—which is probably more than they know.

14 | Training is important; modeling is vital.

When you build disciples, focus more on modeling behavior for them than giving official training or book learning. It's important to move them into the fray quickly. They will more rapidly display the behavior patterns you are seeking to reproduce by doing the ministry with you—and you'll be getting comfortable with them. This is an adult-based training system that works more like apprenticing a journeyman in a trade skill (relational learning) than teaching a class of fifth graders math (top-down learning).

We encourage you to accept the "ready, fire, aim" mentality. The sooner you can get people into ministry, the fewer reasons they can tell you why they can't do it. Once they've done it a time or two, they will be hungry for all the training and education you can provide.

Modeling needs to be enjoyable. You need to create an environment where doing ministry is essentially play. Your team members will not even know they are learning and having an impact—it happens almost accidentally. The members in your church turn in one day from being people who will go from telling you all the reasons they cannot do something to being able to tell you why they can do it and all the reasons it's so cool.

15 | Train leaders like crazy!

Train group leaders constantly.

In order to be ready for the growth that God is going to bring your way, you need to have a ready reserve of leaders. Create a solid leadership environment where almost anyone can try almost anything. It's a "ready, fire, aim" thing.

If you wait until you have the perfect small-group leader, many people will leave your church, because flawless leaders don't exist.

When you train small-group leaders, you also disciple them in your style. Your leaders need to see beyond themselves to the needs of the others in your church. They need to see that it's not just about them getting their needs met but about loving and serving the folks that God brings to your church.

Develop a pool of leaders who are ready, willing and able to take on a group, and you will be ready for the numerical growth that is headed in your direction.

Let everything you do be a double-purposed matter: Do it for the point of doing it, and do it to train someone. Take someone along with you wherever you go. Let them watch you doing ministry. Model your ministry values all the time.

u can do anything else, do it. You're in charge of pennies, not doll
n new church will have a unique way to do the tasks of ministry. Pe
re on; deal with it. Recognize that a very large percentage of the
h you gather will be already-converted people. What do you dr
ut? Is it a big church—or changed people? Lame facilities are OK.
. A lousy attitude isn't. Staff turnover is normal, not a sign of lur
. Begin to delegate now. Have fun on the journey. Don't be pi

ATMOSPHERE

MONEY

16 | **You're in charge of pennies, not dollars.**

One pitfall of good church planters is that they are big-picture people. This is great in most areas, but not for finances. When your people give you money, they are really giving it to Jesus. It's special. You are stewarding money others have tithed. Taking good care of it is a sacred responsibility.

- **Thank every new giver with a handwritten note.**
  How many pastors thank in writing those who give?
  Not many. Yet this is the most sincere form of thanks.
  It forces you to notice people and money you might
  have missed. Do not delegate this job—ever. Once your
  congregation reaches 500 or so attendees, the volume

may become too great to continue writing by hand. But you can still add a handwritten note and signature to a letter typed on church stationery—always do this in your own hand. You will reap many rewards if you follow this simple plan.

- **On Monday mornings, evaluate your giving. Compare Sunday's giving to one-fourth of your monthly expenses.** For example, if one-fourth of your monthly expenses is $2,000 and only $1,900 came in, then you know you need to be vigilant—you have $100 less than you need to pay the bills. Cut back now on expenditures before it's too late. Did you bring in $3,000? Great! Then you only have access to that extra $1,000 for nonbudgeted expenses. The $2,000 base to cover your bills must be maintained no matter what. Don't wait till the end of the month to find out that you can't pay the electric bill or a salary.

- **Please, hire a bookkeeper ASAP to balance your checkbook and reconcile your checking account.** This needs to be someone with no connection to the church, if at all possible. Make a date every Monday to meet with this person and decide how to distribute the money.

- **Always have a bookkeeper open and verify your bank statements.** Don't ever do it yourself! Having a third person involved with the bank statements avoids the most common forms of theft in churches.

- **When you say thank-you to new givers**, send a document explaining the financial controls that you already have in place and an invitation for feedback on any of the issues. Better to discuss any questions up front than to have them stop giving.

If you are not accountable for the small things—paying attention to the spreadsheet on a weekly basis—then you will not be accountable for the large things later.

17 | Create safety around money issues.

We have to understand that there is a reason to create safety. People are concerned when they give money to a church plant. They need to be reassured that they can trust you to spend their hard-earned dollars wisely. They give because they believe something positive can come of their investment. Your job is to make sure that their trust is not misplaced.

Consider having police protection when you get to a size of a couple hundred in attendance.

Here is an idea for building trust: Consider having police protection when you get to a size of a couple hundred in attendance. If you have 150 attendees, your offering could have $600-$800 in cash in it, which is more than enough to be interesting to someone who is checking out the possibility of thievery.

Every single person we've brought up the idea of police protection to thinks it's a crazy idea at first. But there is wisdom in security. We recommend you use an off-duty policeman who is wearing a uniform and a gun. This not only protects your money, but it creates a unique sense of safety for moms and kids.

The policeman can also help with parking or traffic issues during nonoffering times. *Use your police coverage in open areas where money is being transported.*

How To Take an Offering

· **Choose carefully the language you are going to use to talk about money.** Be extremely specific. The most important thing about being specific is you need to honor the not-yet converted in your audience. There are lots of variations of language that you can use. Just be sure you know why you are using that language and use it consistently.

· **Ask not-yet-converted people what they think about the way that you talk about money.** Say, "We try to talk about money in an intelligent way. Are we being successful? Are we being too pushy? Are we connecting?"

· **Use receptacles that don't offend people.** For example, if you use a gold plate with a red velvet bottom at a church plant in Boston, you will turn people off. Gold plates are used in the Catholic churches most of your audience has come from and will offend them. Use a bag or a deep box so that people can give anonymously. People across the United States prefer these types of nonglitzy approaches.

· **Use women to collect offerings.** The more women have visibility in your church the better. A contemporary church plant can't afford to "dis" women in any setting.

· **Don't always have the same people count the money.** This is obvious. There always need to be checks and balances built into the system. Having the same people always counting looks bad and is plainly poor thinking.

· **Have two or more people always do the counting together—never one alone.** Where two or more are gathered together, there is safety and levelheadedness.

18 | Have a CPA do a complete audit annually.

Going to a certified public accountant may seem unnecessary up front, but it is a great investment in the long run. People will demand financial accountability as you grow. Besides, nonprofit organizations that are in financial chaos will rear their ugly heads again and again in the news media. You do not ever want to be lumped with those in disarray. The earlier you do it in the life cycle of your church, the easier it will be for people to trust you.

Don't go to a friendly Christian accounting group that will do a low-priced but probably not-so-professional job for you. Go to a professional. To find a good accounting firm, ask several small- to medium-sized business owners in your city whom they use. You will probably hear one name more than once.

This practice will create an environment of permanence. Churches that are going to be out of business in two years aren't going to do a thorough CPA audit.

We assume that you will do an audit annually. This is a normal part of the checks and balances of leading a church. This audit will also help you when you get to the point of needing a loan for a building or some other major project.

The first time we did an external audit, it seemed like we spent a lot of time and money on the project. I (Steve) thought more than once, *Why are we spending this much money on this expense? No one is being led to the Lord. No one is being loved.* But this activity allowed us to stay in business for the long run.

19 | Avoid unlearned money-repellent behaviors.

- **Failing to present yourself as a respected community leader by the way you dress, the way you cut your**

hair, the appearance of your business card or where your offices are located. Even if you are pursuing urban Bohemians, people still expect a leader to be a leader. You don't have to look like an IBM salesman circa 1952, but you do need to look like a trustworthy adult so you can gain enough trust that people will invest in your ministry.

· **Failing to develop a level of professionalism when you speak**. Incorrect English, inside jokes and inappropriate comments—there are plenty of speech faux pas which can alienate people to the point where they will never return and never support you financially.

· **Misperceiving the way that you interact with people**. You can be Caspar Milquetoast—timid and unassertive—simply because you don't want to alienate people. On the other hand, you can become so arrogant that you convince people that you don't even need them to attend. It is possible to become whiny about money issues. This is just plain irritating after a short while.

· **Associating, hiring or continuing to use the services of employees or volunteers who themselves carelessly commit the transgressions listed above and refuse to change their behavior.** When you discover associates in ministry who spurn correction in these areas, you must address their attitudes and behaviors. If they will not respond to your words, you must clearly cut yourself off from them. Tolerating a working relationship with such people will give the signal that you too are of that same practice or that you have no control over what goes on in your ministry.

· **Ignoring children's church**. You must provide a first-class environment for the children of the families God is drawing to you. Parents are extremely sensitive to the quality of the children's program and the compassion and happiness of the people who run it. They will only endure a certain amount of frustration in this area before they go somewhere that will treat their children better.

- **Forgetting to say thank-you when people do give.** While people are thrilled when you do say thank-you, they are greatly offended when you don't acknowledge a gift. As we noted earlier, we recommend that you thank people with a personal note the first time they give. You should also thank them on a quarterly basis when you issue giving statements.
- **Allowing disorder, clutter and just plain dirtiness.** Take care of your facility. Honor the space God has provided for you. Learn to sweep the room visually before each event to look for clutter, distractions and eyesores. If this is not your strength, recruit a Martha Stewart type who is good with details.

DEMOGRAPHICS

20 | **There must be a match between you and the community in which you serve.**

One of the pastors I coach took over from the founding pastor of a small church in Ohio. The original pastor, who was from an Appalachian background, had attempted to plant a church in an affluent area. In an attempt to reach out to the surrounding community, he sent out 10,000 direct-mail pieces. The graphic on the front of the mailer pictured a man sitting on a chair playing a banjo, stomping his foot and wearing a straw hat. When I saw the picture I thought it was a joke, but it was not. The pastor was making an honest effort to reach his community. He had been attempting to communicate that they were casual, but he

> **Your educational level and the level of those to whom you are ministering need to approximately match.**

ended up communicating something clownish and negative—that they lacked quality. An even greater problem was that in the short text there were no fewer than 27 grammatical and spelling errors! The pastor who followed the founder was shocked when he saw that mailing piece. He seriously considered changing the name of the church out of sheer humiliation.

Here are some factors to take into consideration when seeking to determine a match between you and your community:

- **Education**. Your educational level and the level of those to whom you are ministering need to approximately match. If you are planting a church in a small town in Iowa and targeting a group primarily made up of farmers, you don't need a doctorate in Greek. In fact, that degree might get in the way of your effectiveness in that community.
- **Economics**. Is the financial background that you come from significantly different from that of the people you are trying to reach? If so, there is going to be stress in that relationship.

- **Social matters**. You're going to respond differently to the people of Montgomery, Alabama, than you will to those in Portland, Maine. We have found that pastors from Los Angeles do not usually identify with the interests of the people in Paducah, Kentucky, for example.

- **Style**. Are you going to plant a church in an urban, suburban, uptown urban or rural area? The social style of the community must be taken into account. Each one will have its own unique assumptions toward ministry, language and music.

- **Size and type of vision**. A small-town vision will not work for a big-city church plant; neither will an urban-church plan succeed in a rural setting. There must be a fit.

21 | Get solid demographic information.

Ask any good fisherman what the most important thing is when fishing. He will tell you that it is determining what kind of fish he is going for and what those fish like to eat. A really good fisherman knows how to think like a fish. He will know when they like to eat their favorite food and the best conditions for eating. Therefore, as a fisher of men, whom are you reaching? Where are they located?

Lots of church plants are located near major malls. Here's why:

- There's a pattern of traffic already moving toward and away from the malls.
- Malls are located in areas where population centers are growing.
- Malls are fun to be around—people are attracted to them!

I (Steve) locate most of my church plants near major malls. Significant research has already been done by the mall corporations, so you can rest assured that these are areas that are set in locations that are going to grow in the future. The same holds true for locating near McDonald's restaurants and Wal-Mart stores. If you are located near one of those you are in a growing, high-traffic area.

Get a subscription to *American Demographics* magazine. Ask yourself, *Who am I reaching? Where are they located?*

- Rework the data you receive about your community and your target audience so that other people will be able to understand what is being said. You need to have the information ready so that the average person in your church will be able to grasp your data.
- Be ready to present your data. Arrange it so that if you get an audience with a benefactor, you will be able to present your information in such a compelling way that he or she would be willing to get out his or her checkbook.
- You need to reconcile the choices you've made in ministry and the information you get from demographics. If you learn that within a five-mile radius of your church plant you have a 25 percent African-American and 25 percent Hispanic population, you can't just sing sweet, slow songs such as "Thy Lovingkindness" or old hymns such as "How Great Thou Art." You have to sing something that has more of a beat. If you don't, you'll get nowhere fast.

There must be a match between you, your style and your target. If you and your style don't match, or if you and your target don't match—anytime any of those three don't match—you're in trouble.

The gift that demographic data provides you is real, accurate information on the community in which you are placed. The statistics help you interpret where and who you are. Hopefully this results in greater understanding and improved clarity about where you need to be, what you are missing and how you can improve your dream.

22 | Invite the city to your church.

Jesus has called you to reach your city—not just a suburb, a neighborhood or a few streets. The Great Commission of Matthew 28:18-20 is a call to go into all the world. This is an invitation to think big, humongous, larger than you've ever thought before. Scripture always assumes city-reaching churches, not small neighborhood ones.

God's love is for the city. He is a city-reaching God.

God's love is for the city. He is a city-reaching God. In Scripture it is clear that He is for the church in the city.

When you do servant evangelism, you are making a tacit invitation to your entire city to come to church. In a sense you are inviting them all to the party—that is, to church. The question is, Are we really throwing a party, or are we throwing something more along the lines of a funeral?

Funeral-style churches are marked by a you-must-become-like-us-to-be-accepted-here mentality. One church we know does Communion every week—a fine tradition to keep, but they do it in a very controlling way. The elders run the "show" in such a way that most newcomers feel completely unwelcome and probably laugh at what the church sees as serious business. At the high point of the service, during Communion, the head elder brings his index fingers together over his head. Only when his fingers touch can the other elders begin to serve the elements to the congregation. That's weird! That's a funeral atmosphere.

When the city shows up at church, there are a number of things to keep in mind. If you aren't ready for them, their presence could be problematic with the already-gathered believers.

- **Start early**. The sooner you have new people coming to your church, the easier it will be for your people to include them. When there are always at least a few newcomers, your members will start to expect more.
- **Change things**. Change things for the sake of change. People get settled in very quickly. As soon as they establish a routine, they begin to exclude newcomers. Change will keep the entire system flexible. We do not mean harsh or meaningless changes; rather, modifications that can yield some great fruit to your system. Be ready for how people will misunderstand the process of change. When you see the need to change something, make sure you efficiently communicate what you are doing with those who need to know. Be ready to communicate changes to keep the shock value to a minimum.
- **Welcome newcomers boldly**. Welcome newcomers in a very public and overt manner so that they know you've been waiting for them and that you are happy they have come. You can communicate this when introducing a Sunday service, sending an e-mail or talking to people before and after service. Every communiqué needs to permeate the system with the idea that you are

expecting newcomers to come and they are welcome. This same attitude needs to flow through all of your leaders as well.

- **Catch people welcoming newcomers right and praise them**. Catch people doing it wrong and explain it to them. When people succeed in being inclusive you have to be clear in saying, "That's the way we are going— great job. Everybody follow this person's example!"
- **Love the people that God sends**. God will send people to you when He knows you will love them. We think He is waiting right now to send people your direction until you have purposed in your heart that you will love them powerfully.
- **Be aware**. Your commitment to loving the poor and the lost will alienate a certain percentage of people as well as attract a certain percentage of people. Those values are strong, and they will polarize.
- **Continue reminding your leaders, staff and everyone.** Tell them that the church is about the people who aren't there yet, not about them. Continue to remind them to invite their friends. Your people are a part of the gathering process, too! You start out as the growth magnet, and they'll become the primary growth magnets for new people as you progress.

23 | Start your new work in the parking lot of the most vibrant church in town (or as close as possible).

No, do not literally set up in that church's parking lot; but go as near as possible. Something spiritual, of the kingdom of God, is happening in that place. Take advantage of that reality. At vibrant churches there is a buzz. Catch on to that vibe—resonate with it. For some reason, the wind of the Spirit is happening in that part of town.

Logic would tell you to start somewhere in town where nothing spiritual is happening, but history doesn't bear that out. Take advantage of all the blessings that you possibly can. If that church is a Kingdom-minded place, the leaders won't mind you being nearby. They will welcome your presence.

When I (Steve) started a church in Cincinnati, I located a mile down the street from the obviously most vibrant church in town. The Holy Spirit was at work in that area. People were being drawn to that section of the city. Very few people from that church eventually found their way to our new church, but we benefited from locating in the shadow of that great church.

- Don't try to compete with the most vibrant church in town.
- Don't try to match that church service for service, opportunity for opportunity.
- Pray great blessing on that church.
- Seek to be its friend.
- Always communicate about them with respect, loyalty and affection.
- Get to know the senior pastor.
- Every once in a while, take up an offering for the vibrant church. It can't hurt as you build bridges!
- Invite that church's pastor to speak to your group.

24 | Find your people.

In your city there are people to whom God has called you to reach. They may not be a narrowly defined group. For me it was the disenfranchised of our city—those who were burned out on life and church. They came from a variety of socioeconomic backgrounds, so there was quite a bit of diversity on the surface.

In your city there are people to whom God has called you to reach.

God has a people for you to reach. They have been designed for you—tailor-made just for you. In your city you are the only one who can reach that designated population group. God has raised you up and brought you to your city just to gather that people group.

Pray for a sensitive heart to be able to notice your people. Noticing has to do with an empowering of the Holy Spirit. It goes beyond seeing with your eyes to seeing with your heart.

25 | Find the paradigm for unlocking your city.

God will give you a unique approach to ministry in your city that will mark you and will open the doors of opportunity for you. Your way doesn't have to be unique, but it needs to fit you. For us it is servant evangelism. For you it may be slightly different.

What we can know about your unique paradigm:

• Serving will be part of the key to unlocking your city. Christ calls us to follow in His footsteps. He came as the servant to all. How much more will we be called into that same role? The form that it takes will look unique in each case.

- You will need to experiment with a number of ways of approaching your city before you plant firmly upon your unique way. You need to seek the Lord for a specific approach, for a specific way that will touch the heart of your city. We did a lot of experimenting, and it took several years to fall into the path that has turned out to be productive for us.[1]

- Prayer will condition your heart. Once you have created an atmosphere of prayer in your life, it will be much easier to spot your paradigm. Your paradigm will, more often than not, discover you—then you will discover it. It is common to go through a long dry spell before coming into your paradigm. Paradigm shifts happen when you're grumpy.

- Experiment with paradigms that seem like they might be the ones for you. Just keep throwing them at the wall to see what sticks!

26 | Become one with your people.

I (Steve) had to transform myself into a true Cincinnatian instead of being a Californian who happened to be living in Cincinnati. There comes a time in your move to a city when you become a person of that city. If you believe that God has called you there, abandon your defenses and go ahead, love the people and characteristics of your new community.

I've met a lot of church planters who never mentally moved into their new city.

I met a guy who had moved to central Kentucky from California. He was famous in his new town for preaching against tobacco. That was a dumb move, all things considered. If you are that committed to that stance you need to consider if you are going even near the southern part of the United States. You can't drive down Interstate 75 without seeing scads of tobacco barns. No one would come to his church when word got out that he was against tobacco.

Perhaps nobody told him in advance about the city that he was going to and he went there clueless. Maybe someone had, but he didn't listen. Or possibly he had some level of self-destructiveness. Nonetheless, when he made negative statements about tobacco, it was analogous with trying to leave town and return to California.

Evidences that you are bonding with your city:

- You are not constantly talking about where you used to be. You aren't constantly talking about where you came from.
- Regional idiosyncrasies don't bother you any longer—they don't make you upset.
- Are your kids still talking about how much they miss their friends from the old town they came from? That is evidence that you are talking about your old hometown wrongly at home. You need to shut up and begin to talk differently about it around them.

One church planter that I (Steve) coached constantly talked about the good ole days in California. His children picked up on this sentiment and talked about it nonstop until the family became miserable. They refused to mentally live in Ohio, so they became emotional nomads. After a while it became too difficult to turn the tide, and the family rose up against the church planter, insisting they return to California.

The matter of moving to a new location is one reason you really have to count the cost before you get involved with church planting. When you get there, you have got to burn your boats, as did the conquistadors of Cortez. If you can't choose in advance to burn your boats, then you should not go in the first place.

Lack of love on your part is a cancer that will eat away at the possibility of you being successful.

It bears analyzing that you need to understand how committed you are to a region or city—you have to ask yourself these hard questions, *Do the people of this town like me? Do they like my wife? Am I bonded well?* To not love your city is self-destructive in every way. You will always look back and say, "If only." If you aren't going to love the people in your new city, then why go there?

Is there anything that can stop you from loving these people? If you can come up with anything, you need to face it fast. Lack of love on your part is a cancer that will eat away at the possibility of you being successful in that city.

If you can't see yourself making the community you have selected your permanent home, then don't move.

Trying it out for a season doesn't do anyone any good. You must be so committed that you

- dress like them;
- think like them;
- understand their spiritual background (I [Steve] didn't understand anything about Catholicism before I moved

to Cincinnati, but now I know the lingo and can have an intelligent conversation with a lifelong Catholic);
· understand what they do for fun;
· understand how and why they spend their money;
· learn the top 10 positive and negative things the city is known for—understand them fully; and
· understand the biggest blind spots of the people of the city.

27 | Find your city—the one for which you can die.

After you've done demographic studies, after you've evaluated yourself as to your suitability as a planter, consider these questions:

What's the weather like?

Just kidding! Despite all your physical inclinations, God didn't die for fresh air, green trees and open spaces. He died for people. We must go to where the people are. God has a city for you. It may or may not be the city you are located in now.

· Pray with an open mind. Then pray again. Then pray some more. The key for getting this clarified for you is hearing from God.
· Cities have certain personalities. With some people, when you first meet them, you know you will be close. With others, you just know that no matter how much effort you put into the relationship, you will never fit together. The same is true for cities, so pay attention to your intuition regarding the city you are considering.

- Do you find yourself intrigued at finding unique and fun things in your new city? If so, then you are probably home.
- Check with your family. Do they bond with this new city?
- Think about access. Your city may not be the best in the world, but it may be located near desirable locations.
- Expect God to speak to you in a variety of ways about your new location. This is true especially if fitting in is a concern for you. He'll clarify this matter. Anticipate His speaking to you while you are on the site of your new city.

Most important, once you've gotten the clear communication that this is the city for you—give yourself wholeheartedly to that city. *Don't look back.* This is a city that is marked for you. Your destiny is connected with this place. Put down as many roots as you can. Buy a house when you can afford it. Buy your burial plot there (see number 39 on how to do that).

28 | Identify your kind of people.

Who are you? What kind of people do you like to be with? What kind of people would you like to go on vacation with?

Join groups—bowling, soccer, softball, serving the poor, arts, books, music or whatever is thriving in your city.

Find a gym you like and become a member.

Hang out with people that you like and who like you.

Hopefully your people will include both those who are older and those who are younger than you. In some ways they will be like you; in other ways they will be different from you.

Who needs you and your gifts? Who is hungry for the vision that God has given you?

Your people find you, you don't find them. If you look for them too hard, you will chase them away.

Your job is to share your vision as much and as enthusiastically as possible. From that point on, the people will self-gather.

ATTITUDE

29 | Lame facilities are OK, for now. A lousy attitude isn't.

It is not uncommon for church planters to think that if they have lousy facilities God's blessing must not be upon them. Nothing could be further from the truth. Every great church starts out with mediocre facilities and significant space limitations.

We have heard so many church-planting pastors blame their lack of growth, success or momentum on poor facilities that we're weary. Yes, facilities play a role in a church's success, but it's a very limited issue. More often than not we have found that a church will have a great location with great amenities and very little momentum to show for it. Facilities tend to be an aspect of church planting that receives far too much blame and far too much credit for ministry success.

Before we (Steve's church's) settled in our current facility on the north side of Cincinnati, we met in more than 25 places. Count them—that's 25! Some of them were very hard to find. Some of them smelled funny and we couldn't do anything about it. One place we rented was a karate studio that came complete with a cat that lived there. After meeting there for a month, we concluded that the cat was probably demonized—*no kidding*. When we would pray for people the cat would start to freak out!

Eventually all of this became part of the church's folklore. In the end it didn't matter where we met or how imperfect the surroundings were—we grew in each location. We grew because God was upon us and upon what we were doing. Interestingly, we grew with no advertising.

- Admit it—you can be bitter. Let it go!
- Change what you can about the less-than-ideal facility that has been provided to you. Once you start looking around at the place you have with an objective eye you will realize there are lots of things you can change about it.
- Leave your choice of facility in God's hands.
- Pray and watch for what God will provide. We have found that more often than not God provides breakthrough situations in the area of facilities in the form of invitations. Somehow someone will invite you to look at a building or to see a piece of property. Rarely will the property come to the surface as a result of your independent search. Almost always someone will invite you to look at a piece of real estate that God's hand is upon.
- Prioritize giving over having.
- If you ignore a negative situation, so will others. That is, whatever you do, don't talk about how lousy your facilities are. Your attitude is contagious—for better or for worse. This is especially true when it comes to the senior leader. A bad attitude is also a slap in the face of God, who has provided your current facility.
- Use it up! We (Steve's church) had seven weekend celebrations with 4,000 attendees in a facility that was designed to hold just 500! *Where there is a will, there is a way!* We got creative and found space where the previous congregation had given up and moved on.

- Wherever you are, it's OK for today. Don't spend your energy hating things you can't change right now. Spend it loving people.
- Be grateful for what you have—for what God has provided. Thank God regularly for the facility He has already given you. After you leave your facility, purpose in your heart always to speak thankfully about that place, because in fact God did provide it for you for a short time. Truthfully, if He had not provided it for you, you would not have made it to where you are today. So be thankful!
- Most important: Facilities aren't going to get any better unless you get out and love people. So be quiet, and get out there. Start loving people more!

30 | Personally embody the paradigm of the disciple you are seeking to create in your people.

It's a simple but unalterable truth: Your people become the sort of disciple you embody and present to them as a model. If you want them to pray each day, then you must faithfully seek the Lord in prayer—daily. If you want them to read the Word each day, you too need to be up early each morning reading the Scriptures. If you see your people as lacking in a certain area, you first need to make changes in that area of your own life. Then you may start talking about your experiences in your teaching. This is the only way you will have any hope of seeing behavioral changes in your people.

The people you lead will become what you *are*, not what you *say*. There will always be an anointing on your life *and* actions. We have found that those who just speak a good message but do not live it out will not carry the accompanying power to change lives.

Because we have certain values, there are accompanying activities that we participate in on a regular basis. When we speak on the topics that we live out of our personal lives, they come across as real and authentic because we actually do them. There is power and honesty that accompanies our message in those areas. People can sense our passion and see that

Relationships must be authentic in your life and ministry.

we're thoroughly involved in it, we love it and we do it. They see that passion, and in turn, they want to be involved with us. It's contagious. Where the heart is, there the people will follow.

Take small groups for example. Are you in one? Are they a natural part of your conversation? Or outreach—is that part of your repertoire? Let people catch you doing it and bring them along with you.

Relationships must be authentic in your life and ministry. The questions come up, How do I treat people? How do I handle conflict?

Many famous preachers can communicate that it's important to talk to the lost, but the world has changed around them. The bigger question is, Can they really communicate with those in the culture around them? You have probably observed pastoral communicators who have disdain for the culture instead of possessing love and mercy for it. That is not going to win anyone over. The bottom line is that if you don't model it, they won't get it.

Lighten
Up

These are all contagious matters of the heart. That is, they are all better *caught* than *taught*.

- Care for the poor.
- Love for the lost.
- Love for God's Word—Five chapters a day keeps the pastor away.
- Being a person of prayer.

31 | Don't start something new based on a hatred of the old thing.

Any new thing ought to be what it's for, not what it's against. Never build a vision based on what you are against. Build a vision for the new thing. If you start your church based on what you despise or are against, you are building on a faulty foundation. For example:

- It's very common for new churches that are launched out of a larger, older church to be negatively based.
- Churches with a specific flavor are critically important—Reformation theology, charismatic and anyone who feels they have been marginalized. It is easy to

launch out based on what they are against. This leads to spiritual deadness and a dull atmosphere when the congregation gathers. People somehow know that something is amiss.

Jesus always defined Himself by what He was for. He didn't base His life and ministry on all the ways the Pharisees were wrong. He didn't have to defend Himself.

Over and over again we have found through in-depth discussions with church planters that one of the great hidden mistakes they were committing was making ministry decisions based on not being like something else or someone else. Consistently in those situations the solution to the ministry problem wasn't fixing something in the ministry; it was Jesus mending it in the heart of the leader.

It's also an evolutionary process. You may, a month from now, realize that you have a deep-seated resentment toward a certain group. You may not see it at all. You may experience healing with that situation. A year later, you may experience more bitterness. You say to God, "I thought we already took care of this." But it's evident that there is more to do. Repent, ask for forgiveness, and move on!

evangelism. I liked his comment/question: "I understand that at one point you actually went out and did serving projects yourself. Is that right?" This sincere pastor had obviously come from a theoretical background where pastors don't actually do things—they just talk about them! I was excited to blow this pastor away by inviting him to go out with me right then and there between services. We drove down the street in my Ford truck and went on a toilet-cleaning outreach. He tucked his tie in so it wouldn't fall into the toilet bowl, and we were in for some servant-evangelism action. We cleaned a few toilets and were back in time for the next service. He was no worse for the wear, and he had his world rocked a little bit during the time we invested together.

Do your people a favor by stating ministry goals, values and philosophies in positive ways. If you base your existence on being against someone or something else, it's always a negative deal.

32 | Earn the right to be heard before you attempt to gather a crowd.

The pastor of a well-known, respected church said something profound—if he were to move to a new city to start a church, he would spend at least one year listening to the people to catch their hearts. Only then, having heard their deepest thoughts, would he have the ability to begin to minister authentically to them.

People don't care how much you know until they know how much you care.

Gain credibility before you put out your shingle. You can do this in a multitude of ways.

- Gain credibility through relationships—especially those you establish in small groups and through friendships.
- Serve and care consistently. Through repetitions of service, you earn the right to be heard—that is where people start identifying with you and your church as "the people who care."
- During the first years of a church plant, spend a great deal of your time defining yourself by acts of practical kindness and service. When your people see that you can care for others, they will begin to believe that you can actually care for them.

It always amazes us that church planters are willing to do something costly, such as spend lots of time and money making their church known, but often they are unwilling to do the simple, basic things that produce ministry success. For example, they will spend money on direct-mail pieces, hoping to gather a crowd, or they will assemble a phone-calling crew to contact tens of thousands of people in the community. But they are unwilling to do something as simple as consistently getting out into their community to do practical acts of generosity and kindness. Those who have gone into their community consistently—weekly is a good frequency—have reaped rich rewards. Better yet, why not send out the direct-mail pieces *and* get into the community with lots of servant evangelism!

One pastor has been successful in getting into his community by the simplest of plans. He heads out on Saturday mornings with several wheelbarrow teams. His church members go door-to-door to collect food for their party for the poor that they throw each month. They literally stun people with their offer of simple profundity.

- In the first year or two, one of your priorities is earning the right to be heard.
- Phase 1: When you do it, there is a sense that you don't even need to talk about it.
- Phase 2: The group needs to earn the right to be heard. Do this by exhibiting intangibles that are attractive to people.

33 | Be willing to start small.

One very famous church-planting coach of mine (Steve's) was well-intentioned but dead wrong when he told me, "You can tell if a church plant is going to be successful within the first 90

Press On

days." He meant that all of the telltale signs that allowed a trained eye to determine if the new plant would succeed were present from very early on. This former coach of mine had immediate success as did many of the churches he spun off from his megachurch. My experience has been quite the opposite. With all the churches I have planted and most of those I have coached, I have not found that instant success necessarily translated into long-term success.

Great churches often start slowly. Be willing to move along at a slow pace, especially at first. Often in the early days God is doing a work of preparation to accomplish His purposes. God may well want small for a season. Part of the reason size becomes an issue is arrogance and pride. You can easily get stiff-necked, but God will discipline you severely. There are few things that God dislikes more than arrogance and pride.

If you've had to crawl for a long time before you finally get to the point of being able to walk, walking can be really sweet. I (Steve) had a serious medical accident a couple of years ago that left me debilitated. My legs were completely useless for months, and after an extended time of lying in bed, I had to learn to walk again. It was months before I was able to make it up the stairs. That first trip up the stairs—propelled by my knuckles and arms and dragging my legs—was a great accomplishment. I felt fantastic. As I write this book, I still have difficulty walking, but I will never again take a simple step for granted.

I was similarly thrilled when in Cincinnati we finally grew out of the square-dancing barn in which we started. It was exhilarating. It was thrilling to transition from location to location and from stage to stage for the past 16 years. Starting small is the way that God will likely have you go in His plan for your church. That plan will take you places—the places He wants to take you—so just let His plan have its way in your life. Besides, if you don't surrender to God, you can be stuck for a long time.

> He did the only thing he could do—he moved across town where no one knew him and planted another church from scratch. This second time the plant took hold. He now has some 2,000 people attending each weekend. His is a great story of perseverance in the face of discomfort and downright misery.

34 | Quit quitting.

In the face of great pain it is normal to withdraw from whatever is causing that pain.

Don't get us wrong—it's only normal to feel like quitting once or twice in a year. In fact, if you don't quit every once in a while, you aren't paying attention or maybe you aren't caring enough. But you can't quit planting the church—the task, that is—if a church planter is who you are. You can't leave the city where you've been called.

Most leaders quit planting for the same reason the rest of us quit relationships, jobs, commitments and even marriages. They

Press On

reason, *If I commit to stay, it will require that I face the parts of me that I've refused to acknowledge all of my life.* In Alcoholics Anonymous they call that desire to leave "pulling a geographic." It gets uncomfortable as you begin to see how much you hide and how much Kevlar you've installed in your soul. Friends begin to see your game and call you on it. So you move. The only problem is that *wherever you go, there you are.*

If you stay, you will be humbled, molded and held accountable by people for whom you currently have no respect. You will have deep anguish. You will forever abandon your fairy-tale view of yourself that nobody but you has ever believed. No matter how you try, you won't be able to hide. Does that sound like the job for you? When can you start?

35 | Don't insist on having all the resources in the world to pull off your plant.

We hear statements frequently in church-planting circles these days such as, "It takes $100,000 to $150,000 to start a church." Sentiments such as this concern us because we know they are not true, and we suspect they are scaring away many from thinking about planting a church. We can point to a couple of dozen examples that we have been directly involved with where between $5,000-$10,000 was invested to plant a successful church.

I (Steve) had virtually no money to start the church in Cincinnati.

I am starting new churches right now with an up-front investment of a few thousand dollars.

At the same time, just because you might not have a lot of money to start, you'll sure need plenty before you're through. Know the basic attitudes and behaviors that attract people who can support what you want to build. Somebody does have to pay for this, right? Are you professional, courteous, loving, sensitive regarding time and outward focused? These are all attitudes that make for a successful church plant. Do you dress, carry yourself and speak in such a way that new people would trust you with their tithe? See point 19 for more on this.

36 | Determine to be a life-giving church, not one governed by numerical goals.

Decide what is most important—hopefully to become an alive church that is filled with healthy people—and measure that. Size is a result, not a behavior nor a worthy goal. So you must measure other things and see size as outside of your control. Seeing no growth for a long time naturally should make you wonder, *What's up?* At that point really pray, and seek God to find out what is missing.

What should you measure? New small-group launches, new leaders beginning training, outreaches, "touches" in total, phone calls, thank-you letters, handwritten notes and the buzz (are people hanging around in the meeting area after the meeting, creating a contagious atmosphere?). Are your events helping to

Get Smart

Are you called to plant a church?

Consider the following:

Are you not only called to the task of church planting but also called to this city in particular?

God won't call you to a city on the basis of the nice weather there. There has to be something more substantial to the call. Anticipate something spiritual to happen between you and God when He is about the business of inviting you into a new city.

What does your family have to say about this?

It might be cruel and unusual punishment to move to a new city if your children are in junior or senior high school. Making an entirely new set of friendships at that difficult time in life can be devastating emotionally.

Is there fruit in your life?

Don't go to a new city in an attempt to plant a church if you have not practiced bearing fruit at your home church. Your plant needs to be an extension of the overflow of fruit that you are already seeing with regularity in your current setting.

Do you resonate with the feel of the city?

Every city has a personality—a particular vibe. When you go to visit that city, do you harmonize with it, or does it feel out of sync with you? If you are out of sync, that is no place to attempt to start a church. You might end up fighting a losing battle against the prevailing direction of the city.

Are there enough people to make this plant viable?

Is the population base large enough to be able to do what you want to do with your ministry? If you have a vision to build a 2,000-attendee church but are in a town of just 10,000, you are probably in too small a place unless a major revival breaks out.

Do people listen to you?

Do you have an audience in this new place? In some places you seem to have immediate favor, while in other places it seems that people simply do not listen to you. Before you sign up for the long haul in a new place, discern whether you have favor. Favor is worth more than anything on Earth. If you have it, you can suffer through many ministry challenges and come out a success.

Is there opportunity?

Is there a place in this city for you to make a difference? On the other hand, are you just one of a dozen or more who are doing the same exact thing with only a slight variation of the same ministry? If you are not meeting a felt need in the community, you need to ask yourself if your efforts are worth the price you will have to pay in body and soul.

Do you have peace?

This is a biggie. Without it you can't put your heart into your church plant, and you will not be able to succeed. On the other hand, with great peace and a conviction that God has called you to this place, you will be unshakable and will succeed almost no matter what. It's the peace of Christ that surpasses understanding. It's that peace that will be your strength.

build the community? Finances can be used as a barometer of overall life as well (more on this in number 37).

We recommend you quickly put the scaffolding people to work in servant-evangelism outreaches (see number 8 for the definition of "scaffolding people"). They are often open to being challenged to try new things. We recommend you present the vision of outreach as being normal to these eager people. Present the "new normal" to them that includes outreach on a regular basis. Harness their energy while they are among

Get
Smart

> "Numbers are
> simply a barometer
> for prayer."
> DOUG MURREN

you. They will grow, and your church will benefit.

We've never had numerical goals for the overall size of the church—honestly. We've sought after leadership development goals. We've had group start-up goals. We've desired to stay financially solvent (a very good idea according to our executive pastor!).

Growing? Yes. Very large? Not necessarily.

This is something I (Steve) have had to rethink over the past few years—an assumption I had at the beginning of my pastoral ministry that was faulty. I thought that all churches of significance were destined to be large. Now what do I think? See page 169 where I cover churches of fewer than 500.

So, what should you measure?

- Atmosphere analysis—what is the vibe that is happening around you? What happens to a person from the moment he or she drives into the parking lot until the moment he or she leaves your place?
- New small-group launches.
- New small-group apprentices.
- People in new small-group leader training.
- The buzz—the number of volunteers needed to greet, usher, teach and make coffee so that everyone involved can have fun during the journey and be encouraged in feeling that this is an important thing.
- Stuff that people have to do to be courteous adults.
- Handwritten notes from the primary leader.

37 | Don't take your results too seriously.

In every six-week period, you will have an abnormally high and an abnormally low weekend attendance. You will also have an abnormally high and an abnormally low offering during that time. That's just the way numbers average out. Use the information—don't let it use you. Don't fixate on temporal statistics. At their worst, money fluctuations can drive you crazy. Numbers are simply a barometer for prayer. If the giving suddenly drops, then it's time to go into a time of prayer and ask God, *What are we doing wrong?*

My (Steve's) experience in Cincinnati is a great example of this phenomena. When we (Steve and Rob) met in 1987, the Vineyard Community Church felt like it was stagnating. We didn't think we were getting the traction we wanted. We were having a lousy time. We were learning lessons on servant evangelism and ministry to the poor that were vital, but I (Steve) was still comparing the growth of the local Vineyard church to that of others around the country. By comparison the local church felt like a very slow start, even a failure. As a result, I was angry. After all, I was working hard at church-planting efforts. Luckily, God focused my attention on serving other people outside of the church; otherwise I would have been telling God what a failure we had become. That focus on serving became our saving grace. Before we knew it, momentum picked up. The focus on other people made us attractive to the city. People who are focused on themselves and selfish are unattractive in the most profound way possible. That is death for a church.

Here are some tools to make sure you don't lose focus:

- Invest in a relationship with a person who can confront you. Is there someone in your life who, when are you being arrogant and wanting a large church, can call you on it? Is there someone who can confront you and say that's not what you are all about?

- Analyze what you dream about, what you really want. Journal about it. Be honest with yourself when you are focusing on attendance and money.

- Move away from the "land of Not Enough." Buy a new house—move out of that country. The land of Not Enough is destructive. When you are living there, you can't help but telegraph it to your people in a hundred different ways, spoken and unspoken. God is not mocked. What a man sows is what he will also reap. If

Become an "atmosphere artist"—in other words, build a place where Jesus is warmly encountered.

all you dream about is a big church, that message will ooze out of your pores, and your people will see through you.

- Define what you really want—which is, of course, people who do the deeds of the kingdom of God. Sit down with your team and paint a picture of what your dream disciple looks like. What are you doing now to build that kind of people, and what are you missing? What are you doing churchwide to support this, making sure it happens? What personal commitments are you making that will assure that your people become such disciples?

- Become an "atmosphere artist"—in other words, build a place where Jesus is warmly encountered. Architects are primarily artists—they design things of beauty. The most famous architects design buildings that people never forget. Just as architects bring beauty out of bricks and mortar *to the world*, so church planters bring great gifts that *change the world*. Those gifts are communities that bring the kingdom of God to Earth. The specific

It's easier to have a baby than to pull off a resurrection—and it's a lot more fun!

kinds of beauty can be seen in public services, types of outreach and leadership processes. The church planter has the opportunity to design the atmosphere—that is, the feel, experience and environment of all the various areas of church life. While it's a great opportunity, it's also a large task. One of the most enjoyable points of planting a church is engaging artists who have gifts that can help you with that process. People with design gifts, graphic gifts and music gifts. The role of the church planter is to coach all of these gifted people so that they all make one unified statement: We love you, we welcome you, we want the dynamic life of Christ to shine in you so that you make a difference in the world!

38 | No matter how hard the going gets, remember it's easier to plant a church than it is to resurrect a dying one.

Having worked with thousands of leaders over the past two decades we can safely say that it's more fun and less frustrating to plant a church than to attempt to revive a dead one. While church planting has very little safety connected with it, the frustration of getting old dogs to learn new tricks is much worse. At the conferences we attend, the most miserable people we encounter are those praying for a resurrection of their dead church. The reason for their misery is hopelessness because they have surrendered their dream to people who don't care about the kingdom of God.

So how do you keep your dream alive and kicking for your church plant? Focus on serving. Servant evangelism is a great antivenin for pity parties. Why? Because serving is the fastest way we know to recalibrate in your heart why you are working this hard and investing your life in this church. A simple act of kindness that wants to honor Christ makes everything clear again.

One more thing: You should make friends with someone who is trying to revive a dying church. We think this is a great idea for several reasons. You will probably be able to encourage him or her. Plus, that person will always be present as a reminder to you of how incredibly difficult—no, make that impossible—it is to pull off a church resurrection.

39 | Have fun on the journey.

After being intense on Sunday mornings, I (Steve) spend time Sunday nights unwinding with friends.

- Choose activities that are fun and enjoyable for you. Consider some of the following that other church planters have found to be great unwinding activities: jogging, going to a karate class, playing with your kids, fishing, hunting, watching movies, bowling, softball— anything to truly vacate your mind and get it off of church life.

- Choose an activity that won't let you fixate on what is *not* happening at church.
- People who quit take their results too personally. Don't become a casualty statistic along the roadside of the church-planting highway.

Choose activities that are fun and enjoyable for you.

- You have to take vacations. Get out of town as often as possible just for a change in scenery.
- You have to take up hobbies. Unfortunately we know lots of church planters who stay exhausted with the job of planting because they don't have something else that can take up some of their time and attention.

40 | Be willing to take risks that very well might fail.

This is the attitude that you must have to survive church planting. In essence it connects two critical traits into one small phrase.

Try anything, and try new things all the time. Some people may balk at change for change's sake, but that notion is DNA for church planters. We give you permission to try lots of new stuff. Who else will? The old guard that has done the same things for decades? We don't think so. It's you. You're the hope for people everywhere—that somebody cares enough about lost people that they would risk comfort and try new ideas.

You'll get plenty of chances to become an expert at dealing successfully with failure and rejection. You can't read the work of Paul and miss the failure and rejection he endured to bring

Get Smart

> "Anything worth doing is worth doing wrong."
>
> G. K. CHESTERTON

you half the New Testament. It's also the legacy of all the brave souls since Paul! Anyone who risks enough to share the good news has this trait, too. It may go wrong. Yep, it just might. So what! It probably will. So? Isn't that really God's problem? Learn some new ways to see rejection. Every one who sells must learn this. So must everyone who starts a new business. Think of any sermon illustration you remember. Two of the classics are Edison, who knew 10,000 ways that wouldn't work to make an electric light, and Ray Kroc, who bought a little hamburger stand from two brothers named McDonald. Great preaching is full of stories of courage to be different, honest and true. How about you? How about now?

- When planning for a church plant, think outside of the box. Think extreme! Rich/poor. Fast/slow. Don't assume that your situation will be like anyone else's, and assume it will be exactly like everyone else's, both at the same time.
- Dream big: Find big thinkers, big pockets, big everything. Perhaps Jesus has a gift waiting for you that you never expected. And at the very same time assume you'll be squeezing turnips for a living and that you'll live on faith more than you've been able to conceive. You must be able to live in two separate worlds concurrently and enjoy it. This is why experience counts in church planting. Failure is the tuition you pay to gain experience.

Key: You can't be picky during the first few years of your church's existence.

God showed me (Steve) early on that if I would go after the people no one wants now, later God would give me the people everybody wants.

Failure is the tuition you pay to gain experience.

Church planting is neither for the squeamish nor for the perfectionist. There is so much to the task of church planting that is beyond one's control, it is best taken up by those who can walk with flexibility. As one pastor put it, "Blessed are the flexible, for they shall bend and not be broken." Church planting takes a willingness to step out and try new things. The best planters are those who are part mad scientists (willing to experiment) and part General Douglas MacArthurs (absolutely determined).

But what happens if you fail? Our question back to you is, What do you mean *if* you fail? The church planter knows there is a lot of latitude and a lot of forgiveness, so there is a willingness to experiment to see what will work. The church planter doesn't call it failure. He or she calls it a chance to learn what won't work.

41 | If you can do anything else, do it.

In my (Steve's) moments of frustration during the early days of planting my various churches, I would say, "There must be a more lucrative way to be miserable!"

Like joining the U.S. Marine Corps, church planting is the hardest thing you'll ever love to do.

I once met the business guru Peter Drucker. This wise man told me that he had pondered the relative difficulties of various careers for quite some time. He had come to the conclusion that church planting is the hardest job on Earth and that pastoring is the second toughest job.

It can perhaps seem exciting, even romantic, this notion of going out to forge a new trail, to plant a church. Sure there are elements to it that are positive:

- You can write your own ticket.
- You get to live out the life of a visionary.

But there is probably not a more difficult job to be found, all things considered.

42 | Anger is your number one enemy. Face it often.

Most who are already struggling in church planting are the ones who are unprepared for the high levels of anger that they encounter on their journey. The things that happen to church planters would make an ordinary person upset under the best of circumstances.

When we (Steve's church) first started public meetings, we had a contract to meet at a facility for six months on Sunday nights. Unexpectedly, the fickle school administration decided to give us a one-week notice to leave. We had no leads on a facility. Thankfully, after a lot of emergency prayer was offered up, we found a place within a few days, but that was no thanks to the unreasonable school officials.

If you take the time to launch a church, it will create deep anguish (which expresses itself as anger and hate) when someone leaves, drops off the face of Earth, back-stabs, attacks you, criticizes your marriage or challenges your attitudes.

Expect this series of trials to hurt. The very people who promise to be in this thing until the bitter end will let you down. The changing of these relationships is the primary emotional hardship you can know about in advance. We say that a planting team of 20 to 30 people will have 2 or 3 people left after a couple of years. "Maybe for others," you say, "but not us!" Forget it. We have seen this many times. You will not be the exception. So, how can you prepare?

- Live openhandedly. Don't grab people. Allow them to come in, and allow them to leave. No shame, no angst. Don't keep folks from leaving. If they stay, they'll be bitter and poisonous, and their attitudes will spill over to many others. It's not worth it. Allow people to make their own decisions and respect them—even if you know the reasoning is stupid.
- Learn to truly forgive. Whatever you've known or learned about forgiveness, it will be tested—and then some! Let God mold you.
- Understand the feedback you get from your family. Are you exploding at those you love the most? Are you alienating people who have sacrificed a lot for you? Talk to them. Humble yourself. Ask for forgiveness. Someone wise once said, "The man who doesn't take counsel from his wife is a fool." We agree.
- Believe that you are capable of hate. Church planting is a lot like a marriage in that whatever you bring into it, you'll display more of that under pressure. The passion of the setting will color your emotions.

Over the years we've run into some real spiritual types who don't seem to see themselves as capable of hatred, bitterness or anger. Can you see yourself as capable of these emotions and attitudes? We hope so. This path of church planting brings out some of our basest human qualities. Admit that you hate. God has forgiven lots of passionate leaders over the years—why shouldn't He forgive you?

43 | Come to the amazing convictions that yours is the best church in the whole world and your people are the best in the whole world.

You telegraph your faith and belief to your people in hundreds of unspoken ways. If you've been walking around secretly detesting the people God has called you to, then you have been communicating a vibe that you believe God has given you the raw end of the deal. It's impossible to not communicate that attitude if you hold it. You can't cover it up. It's the simple law of sowing and reaping. You can't fake it. They know.

Your people will also be able to know when that changes. It

The number one reason that pastors fail to enjoy their people is they never train them to focus on outreach.

will change according to how much sleep you get, your blood pressure and the amount of smile time you put out. If you do not love the people, your dream is broken. Your reason for existing can become a nightmare.

What happens if you don't? You miss the greatest blessing that God has for you in life. You pack your dreams in cement and you give them a permanent prison. Until you decide that these are great people, your vision for planting a great church isn't going to happen.

The number one reason that pastors fail to enjoy their people is they never train their people to focus on outreach. Why? Because people who aren't outreach focused are always pests instead of people who go out and make a difference. Here's a thought: If you can just train 10 people to be outwardly focused this year, you will change your church forever.

Remind yourself of this: God has gone out of His way to send these wonderful, unique, odd people to you. The people who come to a church plant are spiritual Rambos. Without them you will not succeed. You can't help but love them and thank God for them.

Acknowledge God's role in who has been brought to your church. Something sovereign has happened in the bringing together of this group of people. Celebrate them.

44 | People move on; deal with it.

If you are located in a large urban area, you have a transient population moving in and out of your church each year. There is going to be an

Have Fun

Servant evangelism is a gathering tool that I recommend building into any church plant. The principle of going out to encounter the community in creative, consistent and compassionate ways is an unbeatable combination. Yet, even in servant evangelism I (Steve) would seek to find my own way. In my various other books—*Conspiracy of Kindness, 101 Ways to Reach Your Community* and *101 Ways to Reach Those in Need*[2]—I have given hundreds of ways to creatively encounter your community. Still, I am convinced there are thousands more untapped ways that we can reach out to our communities that no one has stumbled across yet. If you do a little bit of experimenting and thinking, you can be one of the ones who finds new paths into your community.

automatic 20 to 25 percent annual turnover of people simply due to transfers and career changes. Those are sobering numbers— enough to intimidate even the most resolute of planting pioneers. In order to stay up with the attrition due to job changes and perhaps grow just a little, you will need to add approximately 30 percent more people each year. What a challenge!

When people leave, don't take it personally. A large percentage of departures in your congregation will be just a matter of life happening.

On the other hand, many will leave for other reasons that are not as easy to process emotionally. Studies of those leaving

For the most part, don't take to heart stinging words those departing might say.

churches show that the number one reason for dissatisfaction is a lack of connection with the pastor. In other words, as we have already noted, people most commonly leave because they don't like you. Over the years I've heard it all. "You're not the same as you used to be." "I thought you were going to be a different kind of pastor, but you're just like all the rest." "I thought you really loved me." Don't let the critics worry you. Especially during the first few years you will have numbers of people coming and going as you move toward attaining critical mass, which is 200 to 300 people in weekend attendance.

Sometimes people leave for no good reason. There is no rhyme or logic to their thinking. Perhaps a new church has started, and they decided to check out the latest "happening" place of blessings. For whatever reason, people will be leaving on a regular—make that weekly—basis.

Don't take ownership of these emotional departures. For the most part, don't take to heart stinging words those departing might say, at least not to begin with. If you keep hearing the same comments over and over, perhaps there is a pattern present that needs to be looked into. It is easy to fall into the practice of trying to placate many voices that are seeking to shape you and the church in the early days of your plant. Develop the ability to listen to those voices, smile and then walk on as they leave. How can you really do this?

- Don't expect to be Superman. If it's a key person who you hate to see leave, expect their departure to hurt. Remember, if this is the place that God wants them, they will return. I (Rob) have seen that pattern over and over again.
- Pray. Release to Jesus those who leave. Put them in His hands. Ask for God's best for them. For two weeks straight, pray for them in the same way that you would pray for yourself, and you will usually be successful in letting them go.
- Meet every new person. God is sending you more people to replace those who are leaving. In fact, He is sending you more new ones than the old ones. Don't forget that. Spend quality time with new people. Pour energy into rightly encountering those newcomers (see number 84 for more information on this point).

Do more outreach. Why? Because the focus isn't about the person who just left—it's about the person who isn't at your church yet. The more time you spend obsessing, the less time you have for people who can't wait to be a part of the vision you are birthing. Meeting two or three new people who are excited to begin a journey of faith makes up for a lot of pain. It's even better when they bring along a fresh perspective of what God can do in this new church. It's downright stimulating!

PERSONAL GROWTH

45 | Develop other interests, no matter how difficult it seems.

Most church planters we know are pretty intense individuals compared to the general population. They have a tendency to become obsessive. In particular they can become hung up on the church plant's problems. The idea of developing outside interests is generally a challenge to many of them. To many, having other interests may even seem like a distasteful idea. Building other interests can seem like another difficult chore that has to be done in an already jam-packed schedule. As strange as it sounds, having fun on the journey is not fun for many.

You need to begin to see fun as a normal part of Sunday nights (or if you meet Sunday nights make that Saturday nights). Spend the time unwinding with friends, bowling (so what if you're a terrible bowler—I [Steve] am, and I still bowl) or watching a couple of movies. On most Mondays you will find me (Steve) at Target World—an indoor target range not far from our church where I shoot paper targets with 9-mm pistols. I find this a renewing activity. I often take friends with me on these outings. It's sheer hang-out time with just one rule—we don't talk about church business, unless it's to make fun of church!

- Take time with your spouse.
- Take a day away and go on a date! Writer and professor Eugene Peterson and his wife set aside every Monday to be away from everything. They would pack a lunch and

take a hike in the woods. They wouldn't talk during the first half of the day. They would use the silence to process their life and then stop for lunch and begin to communicate with each other. He reports that this simple act of getting away kept both his marriage and his ministry alive.

- Whatever you do, don't become preoccupied with what's *not* happening.
- Stay active and exercise—you'll need the endorphins! Get a workout buddy if you need one.
- Spend time with people who live balanced lives. Too much time with driven people will only make you more driven. That means that in your free time you won't be spending a lot of time hanging out with other church planters—they are probably as driven as you!

Don't take yourself too seriously—that can happen when you have too few outside interests. We have found that people who quit planting a church have taken their results too personally.

Many take ministry problems as a rejection of their friendship, gifts and ministry. Life is more complicated than that. Every so often I (Steve) quit the ministry—at least for a few hours. When the desire to quit becomes great, it is a sure sign that I'm getting unbalanced and that I need a break from being so intense. At times like that, I to seek out more balance. Take time alone with God. Take a monthly retreat. Get rest. Take time for solitude.

46 | Learn to pray deep prayers.

A deep prayer is something that comes from the deepest recesses of the heart and is directed to the deepest part of the heart of

God. There is no fluff in a deep prayer. This is a prayer prayed in one and two syllable words—sometimes with heavy emotion. Sometimes these prayers include emotion that people who are new to your life may not understand. These are prayers that you pray with veterans in ministry and people you trust enough to introduce to that part of your life.

You'll need them when the going gets rough. Guaranteed.

When isolation strikes, you will, more often than not, be all by yourself. The tool of deep prayers will come in very handy.

Start now! Develop a prayer team that will pray for you, behind you and around you, even before you start to plant. Meet with or just e-mail these people. You'll be glad to know you have their support when the days ahead get rough.

47 | Develop the ability to become what is needed for success.

Sometimes we limit ourselves by the mentality of what we are today. That, however, isn't the way it needs to be. There's no need to be confined by the gifts you possess now. Gifts from the Holy Spirit are situational. That is, as the situation warrants it, God pours them out into your life.

Sometimes we limit ourselves by the mentality of what we are today.

When I (Steve) had a church of 50 people, I had, for example, the speaking and leadership gifts that matched the challenge that was before me. When the church grew, I sensed my gifts were being stretched, so I called out to the Lord and He answered me by raising the level of practical gifting present in my life to meet the level of challenge at hand. When we reached 200 people, for example, He gave me speaking and leadership gifts that were commensurate with that size of the group. He provides as the need arises.

Don't be limited by your lack of gifts. Church planters have the ability to mutate—to receive new giftings from the Holy Spirit in order to be effective at each step along the way.

Church planters possess the gift of reinvention. Morphing is to become what is needed—whatever that might be—to be successful. Like Don Miguel, aka Zorro, on the TV series of long ago, develop the ability to flip your cape over your head and change forms from one person to another.

The experience that church planters have is that the gift appears as you need it. It's similar to the jar of oil that was continually full as it was needed when the prophet blessed the container (see 1 Kings 17:14-16). The more oil that was needed, the more oil that was provided to the container. It works that way with church planters as well. You will be a different person and leader when your attendance reaches 300 than you will be with 50 people. That's just the way that it works.

If you sense that you are in a place where you need to begin to morph, here's what we recommend:

- Take some time away and pray deeply that God will grow you—that God will extend your ability to reach an expanding number of people. Hopefully you will recognize that you are desperate for God to do this. He is the only one who can see this. Whether you can see it or not, God is the only one who can actually do the growing in you.

- Increase your reading about personal, inner growth.
- Increase your reading in specific areas where you think you need the most help. Otherwise deeply gifted people who are having problems with paid or volunteer staff need to have a basic understanding of human resources. Until your church gets to 500 attendees you will be doing all of the hiring and firing. Go to a couple of seminars for your betterment.
- Get around people you have watched morph—people who you are sure know that they've morphed. Ask them who their icons are. Ask them who they learned from along the way.
- Realize that the morphing might be the addition of another person with the needed gifts; i.e., don't be arrogant and think it's always up to you. Those around you have the ability to mutate as well.

48 | Find your coach.

Every successful church planter needs a coach to call upon when the need warrants! This must be someone who has planted a church before you. It needs to be someone who

- cares about your situation;
- gives a rip about how you are faring;
- will get excited with you when good things are taking place and get bummed with you when things aren't doing so well; and
- will support you in heartfelt prayer.

You can't hire people to be excited about your life. God will provide them. You can, however, find people who fit the bill and invite them into your life—that's what I (Steve) have done successfully more often than not.

Most denominational officials in the church-planting office haven't planted a church, so how can they know what they are talking about? How can they give you "been there, done that" wisdom and encouragement?

How can you find a coach? If you don't have one, pray one in.

You need to find a coach of some sort. It should be someone

Hint: Your coach will probably not be in your denominational setting. You need someone who has a set of objective eyes and who can peer into your situation without being clouded by too much knowledge of you or your situation—the coach is not a parent but a peer.

- you respect;
- you enjoy being around;
- who causes you to feel like you can succeed; and
- who doesn't talk down to you.

You will have to invest some money in a coach—that pays for his or her time. But many times people who are good coaches are naturally passionate about people in your role—people, and what they go through.

What's the difference between a coach and a mentor? A coach is interested in the day-to-day stuff of ministry. A mentor is someone you look up to about the deep things of life. Typically you will meet infrequently and for a limited amount of time with a mentor.

A coach doesn't necessarily have to live in the same town. You don't even need to have met that person. You can go with a recommendation.

Tip: Don't waste the coach's time. Be prepared. Know what you want to talk about. Take the time seriously. Differentiate between what's seriously important and what's just frustrating.

Tip: Don't grovel in your situation. There's always hope—that's why you are getting together with the coach. Don't get on the phone and say, "Woe is me." You've chosen to do a fun, wonderful, playful thing. You haven't chosen to do something that requires people to give you money—when you are desperate, don't have anything to fall back on and you want to be rescued, you are groveling.

Tip: If you are going to spend the time to be in the relationship with the coach, at least take his advice. It's better than what you've got. I've been in a number of coaching relationships in which the person I was coaching was unwilling to take my advice. It was sad. They would have been willing to do something complicated if I had asked it, but I asked them to make small, simple changes.

49 | Hear your assignment from God.

Here are our assumptions about your assignment:

- God has an individual calling for each local church.
- Discovering this call is mostly fun. It's seeing the lights go on.
- Your call will be the primary element in the church atmosphere—what makes your church unique.
- It will seep into the experience within everyone in the church.

- It will be a primary drawing card for newcomers.
- It will clearly fit and match the personality of the senior leader and the leadership team.
- Many churches have a call but never discover it. Some discover it but never use it. We think the call is really good news for the church planter who is wondering if he or she will ever make a difference in his or her city. He or she will, if he or she discovers it and follows its lead.

> ## Many churches have a call but never discover it. Some discover it but never use it.

- Your call will fit the people, but it will be beyond where you presently are—it will challenge you to grow to a new level.
- It will always be, at least in part, about people who aren't yet in your church.

Once you get to 200 attendees, you need to figure out your specific assignment. You can't invent an assignment. You probably won't have an assignment from the get-go. God is already preparing you to receive your assignment. Take what He has given you now and run with it. Don't wait. God shows up in mysterious ways. He will likely reach you when you are in the process of doing something else. God is happy to bless any senior leader who is interested in hearing a specific assignment, but so few actually want one.

Don't force God into your timetable. Enjoy the ride!

50 | Find your unique contribution.

Your contribution is not your flavor. For example, to say "We're the people who pray for the sick" isn't legitimate. Everybody should be praying for the sick. "We are the people who move in the gifts of the Spirit." No. Everybody should be moved as the Spirit leads them.

Do something different, unique and outward to define yourself.

How many churches in your area are serving the poor? We suspect zero. Why don't you become the church that serves the poor?

What are the behaviors that you will be known by? Will you primarily be known as monastic, sacramental, outreach oriented, a classroom, a worship experience, a place with great music? All uniqueness is not equal. What you do is your unique contribution. It is not what you think, not your theological opinion or stance, but *what you do*. What is it that you will do so that by your actions the people in your city will know that God loves them?

Have a God encounter. If you just start praying that God will give you one, He will. You may not have a God encounter for two years, but you will have one if you begin to seek after His specific assignment for you in your city.

51 | Get God's heart for the people He's called you to serve and reach.

People come to church for many reasons—some good and some bad. Hopefully many will come to yours because they are hungry for and seeking love, acceptance, forgiveness and a community of kindness. Some come because they love Jesus. Others come because they are looking for a certain atmosphere or feeling. Whatever is unique about your church will drive its atmosphere. People will come because of that extraordinary thing. What is unique about your church?

People will be formed and changed by whatever that unique thing is. Given its importance, the senior leader will wisely expend a lot of energy on whatever sets your church apart from others.

Once you've determined who the people are that God has called you to reach, write down your thoughts about them. What kinds of people like to be with you? You are naturally going to like people who are like you. Good leaders also attract people who are unlike them.

How to start:

- Pray and fast.
- Be with the people.
- Serve the people every day.
- Take your people with you.

"Do you know how to pray that way, how to pray prevailingly? Let sight give as discouraging reports as it may, but pay no attention to these. The living God is still in the heavens and even to delay is part of His goodness."

Arthur T. Pierson

One intangible is that people can tell if you've prayed and discovered anything about the topic you are leading in and talking about.

Pray. Learn everything you can about your people. As you serve them every day you will see a million different dimensions to what they are like. When you serve them and have a place in their world, there is a discovery thing that happens inside you.

As you pray, you will see how your unique contribution to their lives will make a difference in their spiritual lives.

Prayer is trying to link your heart to God's heart for the city.

Discover what your people like. If you didn't grow up in the city where you are planting, you need to do some research. What are they into? What are their politics, dislikes, likes, interests, stereotypes, recreational activities, family structures? In Seattle, you would need to provide worship opportunities that are not focused only on Sunday mornings, because most folks there do not culturally see Sunday morning as church time. Most people see Sunday as a day of recreation, and many go out of town. In Cincinnati, we (Steve's church) asked ourselves, *What is a Cincinnatian?* The more time we spent with Cincinnati people, the more we came to realize that there are many intangibles that go together to make up a Cincinnati person. A true Cincinnatian is someone who eats his spaghetti with chili, is a card-carrying Republican and probably doesn't own a pair of jeans—they do yard work in old slacks!

52 | Teams are good and necessary—just don't overstate their importance.

You don't want to do everything yourself. You aren't a know-it-all. You don't want to get into the habit of working 60 hours a week. So, yes, you need teams. But do not overdo it. We're not suggesting that you do not have a worship team or a team of ushers and greeters. Every church needs those. We're referring to an approach to teamwork that is beyond what is healthy and necessary. Church planters can get too big for their britches.

Some churches have an organizational plan for the team when the entire church is a mere 20 people. The plan for a church of 20 people is "Do you love them?"

- Drop the stipulation that it's necessary to have a team of a certain size before you start or move forward.
- Don't spend too much time caring for and nurturing teams at the beginning of your church plant.
- Teams are to produce work for the good of the whole. They are not to rob energy from the whole.
- Teams can easily become tail-chasing entities and ends unto themselves.

It is common for church planters to become team centered and sometimes to become hamstrung with all that comes with maintaining relationships with the team. Church planters on their own are usually multitalented and multifaceted individuals. Don't underestimate your skill level.

The wise church planter gives away leadership opportunities, slowly naming people to positions of leadership. If you by yourself can do a number of things decently—worship, teaching and leading—then do it at first.

When do you name others to official ministry positions? If you are a male, talk to your wife. She will know the timing of when to name people to ministries. Generally women intuitively know the timing of things far better and more accurately than men. If you have your doubts, then wait a few months before giving away authority to teams. If you are a female church planter, chances are you have a built-in gifting about timing. Use that inclination to your advantage.

We have noticed that sometimes when you name a deacon, they simply stop deeking! Don't forget, if they are bugging you to get a title, watch out.

Teams turned inward are always toxic. In the early stages of a church plant, we've seen teams become black holes absorbing all the energy that comes around them and giving little or nothing back in return.

53 | Get a good therapist—now.

This point could be number one—and maybe it should be.

Point one: Set your appointment. Point two: Don't miss your appointment.

It may be the most important one hour you have that week or month. It's no shame to be under the care of a therapist—it's just good realism and clear thinking.

Many church planters tend to be the rugged-individual type. Perhaps the idea of a counselor seems incongruous to your view of the way God moves upon people and heals their souls. From my (Steve's) own experience there are some issues that simply are too large to take on by oneself. There are some issues that are too complicated to accurately process through apart from the intervention of an outside, objective mind that has a loving interest in the situation.

If you don't need a therapist now, you very well might need one before you go much further down the path as a church planter. Before long you will have experienced significant rejection. Rejection does many cruel things to the human soul. If left untreated, deeper problems can result, which are more complex and more difficult to address. (See point 54 for more on professional counseling.)

54 | Form a group of people who can and will say anything to you.

Church planters can be intimidating types. You need people around you who can say anything to you at any time. You need people near you who are not afraid of you.

It's critical early on to be able to hear the bad news from somebody. That's important because the sooner you hear the bad news, the sooner you also will be able to hear the good news.

We assume that church planters are loners and are mute. That is, they struggle, and they don't share about what they are going through for fear of being labeled whiners. That pretty much describes the people we've coached who have been planting churches. That's why we recommend that church planters both have an accountability group and get professional counseling. If we have a group of mute loners, we need a group of people who can say, "Hey, open up a little bit." You need a break from the fight.

As coaches, we have been able to be a voice that has spoken into the lives of a number of church planters who have become stuck in loneliness. We have spoken into their lives when they were at a point of crisis.

As I (Steve) look back on my own experience, I wish that I had gathered more trusted friends around me to share the emotional burden of the church-planting task. Also, if I had endeared myself to some other trustworthy church planters and business leaders who were able to keep confidences—people who were able to relate to what I was doing because they were also experienced at managing people—I would have fared better. Personal sanity, family issues and life balance are a few of the areas where I needed help. I needed someone to come along at various points and say, "Relax—God's handling it. It's going to be OK." I was too intense most of the time in the initial stages of the planting of my church in Cincinnati, and my body, soul and relationships paid the price.

So, if I can offer any advice in this area, it's relax, make friends, listen to them, and listen to your gut. If your gut says, "Listen to them," then you'd better open your ears. These are people who are hanging around your life—regular people. They are mentors and coaches in whom you can confide; they are outside your geographical circle and won't be affected by what you have to say.

If you can't listen to the first group you attempted to gather, then look again—find others you can talk to and get advice from. They will play a vital role in your life.

55 | Develop an indomitable spirit.

At first glance, this point and the previous one may seem to be in direct contrast with one another, but actually they complement one another.

When I (Steve) first came to Cincinnati, I faced a tremendous rejection rate. The numbers shook me thoroughly. At that time I began to wonder if I had rightly heard God when I first felt led to come to Cincinnati.

You are selling a dream—one that no one in your community has ever dreamed.

When the going gets tough you are faced with two opposing options. You can either bail out and quit, thus never finding out what the potential of your church plant is, or you can commit yourself thoroughly to what is going on and to where the ship is headed.

The life of a church planter can seem like a long string of rejections. That is the nature of being the lead person in a start-up enterprise. You are selling a dream—one that no one in your community has ever dreamed. If you are selling it right, you are explaining your vision this way: "This will be like no church you've seen before!" It is difficult for people to grasp that sort of image, so rejection comes easily.

What do you do when the inevitable disappointments occur? To fight those times is very draining. Sometimes the stress comes from people near by.

We recommend that you do the following:

- Watch movies regularly to counteract the negative effects those encounters can have on you. View heart-encouraging movies such as *Gladiator, Braveheart, It's a Wonderful Life* and *Shrek*.
- Take a walk at the mall.
- Play with your kids.
- Go to the park.
- Get away from asphalt and get close to nature.
- Have a true Sabbath.
- Rest!
- Read a book that has nothing to do with anything connected with church life.

James Collins in *Good to Great* found that what he calls "Level 5 Leaders" have profound humility and dogged determination.[3]

You need partners and cotravelers who will go to the mat for you—who will do whatever it takes to help you win.

You have to "out ugly it," as my (Rob's) dad, Bob, always said. You have to get tougher and uglier than it is—it, of course, being any obstacle or disappointment. Assume that at some point everyone will abandon you. You will have to have faith that you can endure, and you will hang in there with God alone. You will have a challenge that will go all the way down to the center of your soul.

Your ability to deal with conflict will be tested. If you feel that you have to be friends with everybody—if all situations have to be conflict free—then you will fail.

Make a commitment to act lovingly to all people no matter

Press On

what. Commit to your priorities and to life in Christ, and act in a loving way. No matter how much you've been urged to go for blood, don't do it—and you will be urged to do that a lot, guaranteed.

56 | If you don't do outreach alone, then you don't really believe in it.

You want to build lifestyles, not ministry platforms.

If outreach isn't the first point in your discipleship model, it will be no point in your discipleship activity. By "you" we mean the senior leader as an example for the rest of the flock. You must make outreach the main point, then add discipleship, Bible reading and witnessing, or you will start with an incomplete picture.

Don't get us wrong. We don't want you to do outreach alone. But if you don't self-generate opportunities in doing outreach—seeing opportunities and taking advantage of them—your church won't either. That means, if no one came to the party, you'd still throw the party because that's the right thing to do.

You must be a model and show the way for others to follow. It's not someone else's job.

We want to build disciples of action. One of the most critical ways of building disciples of action is for the senior leader to be involved in action-based discipleship. This isn't something that can be delegated. Become the paradigm of a disciple that you are presenting to the people—and do that consistently. You become what you want others to become. You embody what you want them to be.

Don't do outreach or ministry to the poor for show, but do it because it's the right thing to do. It must be authentic through

Make a commitment to act lovingly to all people no matter what.

and through. If it isn't, people won't buy into it. They'll give it lip service but won't follow up. If outreach is authentically inside of you—it's something you really want to do—then you will do it. Your attitude will come out all over the place. You can't hide it.

Pastors and church leaders are normally people who talk and postulate about things. When the senior leader acts instead of talks, it shatters people in the best sense. It is disarming. It destroys the negative religious experiences, rules and rituals in their lives.

On a typical weekend, I (Steve) take people out with me between services to do servant evangelism. It blows their minds that even though I am speaking, I leave the church's facility and go out to do outreach. They came to church simply to sit through a good sermon, sing some songs and go home—no worse for the wear. I am able to rock their world significantly by going out at 10:00 A.M. to do servant evangelism.

At any stage in this process of planting and growing this church, I could have stopped doing servant evangelism, but I didn't. Why didn't I stop? What was the heart character?

I've heard a number of threats and confrontations from people who told me why I shouldn't do outreach any longer:

- It's unbecoming of a pastor of a church of this size.
- Don't you need to pray? (But I've already prayed; besides, being a disciple has to do with outreach more than inreach.)
- Your church is big now, why would you do this?
- Don't you have someone else in your church who can do this? (You can't delegate a primary responsibility.)
- Don't you need to rest between services?

When you start with outreach, expect to do it by yourself more often than not. Consider your solo outreach times as meditations between you and the Lord. When you begin to gather a group, pray that they will be God sent. Pay close attention to the lessons you learn in your early days of outreach—they will be spectacular lessons that will be vital later. Get the resources you need to do an effective job—attend a conference that will help you do outreach effectively; pick up some books on servant evangelism that will help you be as effective as possible.

Your enthusiasm for what you are doing is important because it creates the atmosphere for the whole experience. Be sure to follow up on the people you take with you on outreaches. Journal about the outreaches—whether you are alone or with others. Determine in your heart to gather all the gifts that God gives you along the way—insights, heart changes, mission statements, convictions and Holy Spirit experiences.

57 | Build your faith.

As you have seen, negativism will creep into your path as you step out to plant a church. To avoid letting this rip you apart, ask God for the gift of supernatural faith—the kind that can move mountains. You will need it. He delights in giving greater faith to those who seek it.

- Spend time with people who have the gift of supernatural faith.
- Spend time with people who have successfully done church planting. Absorb their encouragement. Veteran church planters are typically encouragers because they know how difficult a task church planting is.
- Stay out of the negative—this is critical.
- Regularly pray and fast for extended times. That transports you into a place of being able to see from God's perspective, giving you a glimpse of what He is doing instead of only seeing what is going on at an earthly level.
- Maintain consistent access to children. Stay around little children because they believe anything and everything—the sky is the limit with them!
- Take time for yourself to do the things that connect you with God, whether it is writing, walking, reading or something else. Make the time. Make it an appointment and put it into your regular calendar.

58 | If you are coming out of a hurtful, disappointing church experience, get the help you will need to get past that negative energy drain.

It's a given that you will go through painful church experiences. We've all been through more than one of them. In other words, it's not a matter of *if* but *when*. If you look at successful churches, you might be tempted to think that the leaders have not suffered through any disappointing ministry experiences or that the success of the churches makes up for all that pain. It doesn't. Begin today to build the skills that you will need for the rest of your life and ministry.

- You are going to need someone whom you can say it all to. Note: That person doesn't live at your house. Do not burden a spouse. Seek out a therapist. The more comfortable you are with yourself, the easier it will be for the people in your congregation to relate to you and accept your leadership. That is, whatever price you pay for wholeness will be worth the cost because of the benefits that will come about as a result.

- Develop a new community of friends. This is not only necessary for your ongoing mental health and general happiness in life, but it also makes planting a church a lot more fun.

- Accept responsibility for your role in whatever bad experiences happened in the past. Don't focus on the other guy's mistakes—pay attention to yours. If you need to, go back to the people in that situation or situations and ask them for forgiveness and feedback regarding your role in the bad experience. If there is still someone at the organization whom you can trust, do an exit interview on yourself. Find out what you could have done differently to have kept the situation from ending as badly as it did. Seek insight on what you could do differently the next time you face a similar situation.

- Bad situations affect your family. Expect some well-deserved "I told you sos." Expect kernels of wisdom from small people (your children).

- Don't begin planting a church until the effect of the bad situation is truly history, and you can deeply utter, "I'm over it."
- Don't allow yourself to talk about the old situation more than 15 minutes per day.
- Decide you won't use the "__" word again. Refuse to let the negatives in your past dominate your future.
- The people in your new church don't know any of the people from your previous situation. They don't want to know about it. They don't care. Do everyone a favor and don't talk about it in your new location. It will do no one any good. Instead, it will likely do harm to many souls. The people at your new church just want to know about how you are going to love them.
- If you are working on a preplant, get to a good place in your own life before you start. If you are in the midst of a plant, understand the need to deal with any past hurts and get them behind you. Work at it like it's a job. It's like stump removal. It's dirty, hard work, but it's completely necessary if you are to eventually have green grass.
- Set a deadline—a date when you intend to have this situation behind you. Our assumption here is that the ending date will be months or a year away, not weeks. Don't rush things. If you do rush things, you will only fool yourself into believing that you are past the hurt when, in truth, the bad situation still lurks just beneath the surface of your emotions.

STRATEGIES

59 | Don't seek to be original.

Someone once said, "There once was a man who sought to be original or nothing. In the end he was both." No one is really original. If you listen to the tapes of well-known pastors around the U.S., you will discover that they inspire one another. Their weekend teaching lessons follow each other.

You will gain the respect of your community or lose it based on the quality of your communication pieces.

There are so many resources available for sale—worship tunes, PowerPoint presentations, drama skits, software for putting together a service and lots of powerful sermons. To generate things from scratch is actually not so smart an idea for the beginning church planter. It boils down to a simple matter of time. Be efficient. As the planter, you are the small-group starter. You are also the primary therapist for the church and the preacher week in and week out. There's just no possible way that you will have the time to generate all those things from zilch.

- Songs and worship. Check out resources such as vineyardmusicusa.com, integritymusic.com, maranathamusic.com and sacramentis.com.

- Leadership training materials. You will find plenty to work from at: injoy.com, willowcreek.com and regalbooks.com.

- Graphics. Borrow logos from places that you like (if they are not trademarked). Borrow others' mission statements until a better one comes along (if they are not copyrighted). You have our permission to borrow; however, if there is a trademark or copyright, ask permission. Most pastors will help others. Be blessed and borrow! A great site that is worth visiting is churchwerx.com.

- Weekend message. A church-plant pastor has at least 50 different tasks and doesn't have 35 hours per week to prepare for a message. This is the ultimate reason why you need other people to help you. You need help with your message. If you are using your time correctly, you will be adapting other pastors' messages the first few years. It's helpful to have a basic framework that has worked for someone else and build on to the essence of that message with your own stories and life experiences.

Get Smart

When we first got into the arena of websites, we attempted partially to design our own site and partially to get someone else to do the job for us. We spent months going back and forth discussing the logo, the look, the feel of the site. We probably poured a hundred hours of meetings into the project. After nine months of a frustrating cooperative relationship, we decided to beg off on the relationship. Mind you, we had no website to show for all of our discussions. We had nothing. Our bill for those discussions—a whopping $15,000! That wasn't exactly what we were expecting. The lessons we learned on that exercise (which was probably worth the 15 grand) was that we should hire someone to do the work and be done with it. It's vital to give input at the beginning of the process, but then let them do their job. Our "help" cost us most of that money and we deserved the sticker shock we got in the end.

You probably don't have a strong enough, unique enough message to begin with. Don't worry about being original. On the other hand, you can't afford to do a mediocre message. Check out the resources of some of the best communicators in the country, such as Rick Warren and Bill Hybels at pastors.com and willowcreek.com.

The greatest cost you will have will be in the area of communication. You will be judged and evaluated by the community on the basis of how well you communicate in all means of media. You will gain the respect of your community or lose it based on the quality of your communication pieces. Therefore it is of the greatest importance that you spend the appropriate amount of time, money and energy invested into these various media so that they accurately portray your group's persona.

Someone else should be doing everything for you except what you really need to do. Perhaps the only thing you can't entirely hand off to someone else is the message. Practically every other aspect of the weekend celebration can eventually be delegated away from you.

Each new church will have a unique way to do the tasks of ministry: small groups, worship, leadership development, outreach, discipleship, preaching and others.

Don't force the style from your former church upon the new group of followers you are developing. If they wanted the other ways, they'd go to the other church. They know this new church will be different. Your people won't make you apologize for the differences. How can the new church be the same as the former? It's not possible. You aren't the former church. It's as simple as that.

Know that the form of your church plant will evolve over time, and you may, for example, have no small groups for a season or two. This is a new thing you are shaping. The way you did almost everything at the former church—in small groups, in the service and so forth—is all up for negotiation. This process hurts, especially when you're

Find your own way, then allow it to be truly new!

ultracommitted to a particular way of doing something, but it's how Jesus gets what He wants! Keep in mind that He desires to do a new thing in your church plant. The tough creative environment of a start-up automatically generates new ideas and new ways of doing ministry. Larger, older churches don't struggle for their existence. Your struggle is the crucible where God forms all the things that make church planting rewarding in the end. Forcing your church to look like others defeats His intent of creating new tools and new ways.

It's good to have models, but don't be bound by someone else's model. David tried on Saul's armor. Fortunately he had the good sense to take it off before he went into battle with Goliath. If he had kept Saul's armor on the story would have ended very differently. But David *did* try the armor on. And he walked around in it for a while. He certainly felt that it was wrong. It works the same way with church planters. It's OK to try another's armor on for a while.

Winning wasn't optional for David, and neither is survival for you. The result of losing for David would have been death. That was his filter—his ability to understand whether the armor he was using would help or hurt his cause. As church planters our task is similar. We must filter the useful from the not so useful. On occasion we use new things (a slingshot) and at other times old things (Saul's armor). For us spiritual life and death

Show Love

hang in the balance. If you filter all your choices through the grid of giving spiritual life to your city, you will choose well.

As an example, at Vineyard Community Church in Cincinnati we had to let go of our model of "kinships," or small groups, as we experienced them for quite a number of years in our former church. The way we had done them had become a sacred cow. My wife, Janie, and I (Steve) brought from California a model for doing small groups that was very exacting and inflexible. It was *the* way to do small groups. It became obvious after a while that this style of ministry wasn't working any longer and that it needed a significant revamp. After substantial pain, adjustments were made to the small-group structure that were necessary to move forward. That process has been repeated a number of times with small-group ministry.

It's necessary to hitchhike on others' methods and models to get started, but after a while you have to adjust, change and find your own way.

- Allow a church plant to be truly new.
- Go with something tried and true, but be open to change.
- Get feedback from other people.

- When you are talking about planting a church, you need a balanced group of men and women. In the past, church plants were often male dominated—but no more. If over 50 percent of those you seek to reach are women, then members of both genders had better be a part of the planning team.

61 | Realize that no one will be the final decision maker for this organization—*but you.*

Of course, Christ is the final authority for everything, and the Bible is the final authority on all matters of faith and conduct. But when it comes to leadership and making practical decisions about the life of the church, *you* are it. Someone has to be the buck stopper.

There is a team aspect to all ministry. The church doesn't work well without teamwork, but someone ultimately has to step up to the plate and be the leader. There's nothing more frustrating than being a part of a group that is weak due to leaderlessness.

The word we use for leaderlessness is "abdication." In a hundred ways in the life of the local church, most senior leaders abdicate their role and allow others to choose for them. If you plan on planting an effective church, you must be able to

with some degree of effectiveness. The community took notice of these practical works of love and generosity. Instead of fading into the backdrop of the cityscape, they stood out as a clear and unusual beacon. What were the results of this experiment in generosity? Five years have passed and they now average 500 in Sunday attendance. Not bad considering they started from scratch. Their success has been so dramatic that their entire denomination in Florida is adopting servant evangelism as the means for launching all their church plants.

own the role of decision maker. As the decision maker, you will intentionally make the call in most areas of ministry—especially when your church is very young. No amount of delegation reduces your responsibility. No matter if another leader has impeccable credentials, superintelligence and the wisdom of Solomon, it is still your job to make sure that what you intend is accomplished in that ministry. Being a leader who accepts this responsibility makes you a lightning rod for conflict. From our point of view that conflict is a gift. It is an opportunity to stand your ground because you will have opposition to every important decision that you will ever make. Sometimes the ones that seem small will be the most important. For instance, what if you decide that 5 percent of your income should be spent on serving the poor? Do you think that that will create some conflict? Most definitely. At some point those who serve with you will recognize that you mean business about your dream—that you fully intend to see it implemented. At every turn in the venture, people have to decide if they want to paddle or jump ship.

62 | Be yourself! Don't be intimidated by the supersuccessful models of the giant-sized churches that are all the rage today.

Churches of 10,000 or more in weekend attendance is a new phenomenon on the American church landscape. While this is an exciting reality, these oversized churches can be intimidating to church planters who can inadvertently begin to think that this is the norm in practice or size. Each megachurch has its own success story and personal secret to go with it. The task seems so easy when you hear how that church did it, but truthfully there is rarely a single second church that has a fraction of the success the original one had using an identical model.

Can we learn from the originals? Sure—there's plenty to glean. Good counsel, however, in general is not to try to imitate them.

For the most part, a megachurch is one-of-a-kind. For that matter, all churches are!

> ## Don't rush into your church plant. You're not a miracle worker. Let God build the house.

We have seen so many leaders struggle for years to sell the sizzle and not have any steak. They feel that if their church doesn't have all the ministries and features of XYZ church, they are essentially failures and have somehow let God down. Doesn't that sound like a lie? Have faith that God knows what He is doing.

Don't rush into your church plant. You're not a miracle worker. Let God build the house.

I (Steve) have found that as I do servant evangelism, the intimidation I have sometimes felt by these churches is often displaced by the joy of what God adds to me by service in the community.

Once, when I had gone through a particularly difficult time, two couples who had been with us from the early stages of the church informed me in a not-so-delicate way that they no longer followed the vision that we were pursuing. They said that in fact they had never really bought into the vision and considered the entire time they had spent with us a complete waste of time. They were leaving to go to a cool, happening megachurch across

Lighten Up

town that promised to be everything they wanted. What a slam dunk! They left and kicked the door shut on the way out.

This all happened on a Friday before I was to speak on the weekend. I needed to be completely up for the services. Although I am fairly used to people dissing me, the departure of these two couples sent me for a loop. Going into Friday late afternoon I felt weary, so I went on an individual servant-evangelism project to try to adjust my attitude. I went out cleaning toilets at gasoline stations and fast-food restaurants. It was amazing. By the third stop my spirits were lifted and my mood had completely shifted. Such is the power of being outwardly focused even in times of darkness. The only solution is to get back on the horse that bucked you off.

Focus on serving: It's a great antidote for pity parties!

Your success will vary greatly depending of many factors. Just remain faithful to doing your rounds in the city—continue to go out among the people to whom God has called you to minister faithfully.

Your success will also have something to do with the city in which God has placed you. Some cities are tough, while some are easier to crack. Some have a season of readiness. Where is yours right now?

What kind of people has God given you to minister to in your city? Some are more challenging than others. We all have different assignments in the Kingdom. It's a matter of knowing what God has called us to and faithfully carrying it out. Some assignments clearly are more challenging than others—I know that from the experiences that I've had firsthand in planting four churches.

Your gifting will have a bearing on how easily you are able to release your calling to your city. If you are greatly gifted and the challenge level is not that great, then the matter of planting with some significant momentum should not be as great a challenge as if the situation were reversed.

63 | You can launch public meetings sooner or later depending on the skills, experience, finances, depth and confidence of leadership team.

I have heard a number of formulas for knowing when to go to public services. Those figures range from 150 to 300 attendees. I've found that it's possible to successfully make the jump to this important point with just a core of 40 to 50 people provided there are enough resources to meet the needs. Aubrey Malphurs and Joe Aldrich, in their great book *Planting Growing Churches for the Twenty-First Century*, advise that if you have a core group of 50, you will have the potential for unlimited growth with your group.[4]

There are several factors to take into consideration regarding how soon you go to Sunday-morning meetings:

- Leadership within the various ministries of the church.
- The up-front speaking skill set of the lead pastor.
- Momentum inside and outside the church. Are people in the surrounding community curious about this new thing?
- Adequate finances to hire quality child-care workers and musicians.
- Training for other people to be able to greet, usher, help with transitions and run the technical aspects of ministry.

Honesty about what you have available is vital. Be realistic when it comes time to evaluate the readiness of your group to go to weekend celebrations. You won't have ministry available to everyone. Be honest about it. Communicate to your people that you're a small church. We've known plenty of people who have communicated, "We have ministry available for everybody," and they ended up being embarrassed. Don't make that promise. You will simply look silly.

64 | Make a 10-year commitment.

Step 1: Buy a burial plot.

Step 2: Make frequent reference to that burial plot as you talk about your commitment to your city and to your people. (If you place the headstone in your living room, it makes a heck of a conversation piece!)

We find that church planters commonly think, *Well, I'm here for now. I'm here until something better comes along.* Perhaps it is part of the emotional makeup of the kind of people who are drawn to this type of ministry. However, the truth is that nothing better will come along. That sort of shortsightedness will not produce good fruit.

If you are constantly reexamining your commitment to either the task or the city in which you are serving, you will be continually assaulted by the enemy. Make a commitment and decide not to reconsider that decision for a decade, then get to work.

If you haven't settled that issue, then you telegraph your indecisiveness with every pore of your body to everyone around you. You end up saying, "I'm not home yet." You can't be a port in the storm for hurting people because you are still a moving target. Such a posture is a primary sign of ministry immaturity.

Here's what we recommend: Put away all thoughts regarding leaving for 10 years. Put it in your Palm Pilot for 10 years from this month: *Reevaluate my commitment to this city*. That's what I (Steve) did. Then years later I saw that note and laughed. I was spending so much time serving the people of the city that all I could do was chuckle at the ridiculousness of leaving. Why 10 years instead of three? Ten years might as well be forever.

65 | Spend your time in the right ways, especially in the early days.

Gather, gather, gather, gather, gather. Tell your story, then tell it again and again and again. Get out with the people. The book of Acts has numerous references to the apostles being among, or with, the people day after day. It is our role as well to be among the people of our city if we hope to make a connection.

- Develop leadership. Use turbo groups (see glossary).
- Clarify your vision. Assimilate it. Explain who you are and why you are here.
- Don't spend too much time on message preparation.
- Don't spend all your time at church—get a job, especially in the early days. When you first start, there's not enough to do to occupy you full time. Even if you can afford not to work, still get an outside job. Later you'll be glad you did.
- Don't spend your time being frustrated—don't dwell on what's not right with the church.
- Don't spend your time pining away for the good ole days—when you had money and you didn't have to do everything by yourself. Those days weren't that good anyway, and there weren't that many people helping you out.

OK, so what should you do?

- Pray—really hard. Don't pray-whine but pray, truly pray.
- Gather continually, habitually, every day.
- Pray some more.
- Read Scripture.
- Serve perpetually.
- Have coffee, build new friendships, build new networks.
- Read—stay fresh.
- Write. Before this church plant is over, you are going to be a proficient writer.
- Develop leaders.
- Clarify your vision.
- Assimilate like crazy the new people coming into your new community.
- Do outreach in a variety of creative and consistent ways.
- Build your own life. Decide what kind of life you want to have and build it. Get a coach who will help you have the kind of life that you want to have; then pursue it vigorously.
- Have hobbies.
- Build personal interests.
- Spend big chunks of time with your family.

Understand that there is going to be a delay between the point when leaders show up and when they are effectively in place and serving.

Much of the initial leadership help you'll receive will be from friends who are excited about your vision and have done well in the business world. They are Rambos—they ooze enthusiasm! Unfortunately, much of their success and passion doesn't transfer well. They need to be trained about the pressure and weight of ministry. That weight may be the ultimate burden. If they don't have any experience, it will take a few years until they "get" what's really going on. Train them now to avoid as many bumps as possible.

This training period also starts a process of each leader making an under-pressure decision to stay and fight. Get it over with! Do leadership training early, even when you're sure you don't have time! Many of the people who say they want to help won't when you explain what you really mean. Let them leave. This is best done before you begin public meetings. Be tough. Tell the truth! Better to have them vote now rather than later when they have significant responsibility. If they leave further along in the church's development, you could be left in the lurch and "out" someone you considered a friend.

This is true for all the leaders in a plant, not just the senior pastor. Once all the leaders have been let down a few times, they'll realize how gross it would be if they let others down. And that's a good thing! Until this happens your team hasn't been tested, and you don't know if they really will endure the tough times. Church planting may have created more ex-best friends than anything else! Remember:

- Letdowns are permanent! Yes, this dynamic continues as the church grows for its entire life.
- It's natural! It's the rare human in any culture who will say, "You know, I've been thinking and this doesn't feel right. I have many more bad feelings than good ones. I'm starting to be unable to hear you when you communicate from the Bible, and I feel like I want to do everything different than you do! You wanna get a latte

and talk about it? I feel so bad." Sorry, but you'll never hear that. If you ever do, please call us. We want to meet this person! But even if that happens, you still lose a valuable team member. It hurts!

When someone decides to leave, you must honor the loss. This is one of the worst parts of ministry and life. But once you've processed this, you can begin the most important part of this process. A space is open. Work needs to be done. God is calling someone new. It's time to recognize that person and to start

When someone decides to leave, you must honor the loss.

slowly honoring the new development process Jesus has already begun. It may feel like there is nobody who could *ever* take the place of the person who is leaving. But there is. And the new person is usually invisible until the old one finally exits. It's a strangely wrapped gift, but a new gift nonetheless.

67 | Don't put people in charge of things too early.

It's easy to put people in charge of things. On the other hand, it's messy, difficult and tedious to take them out of positions. It's a simple matter to hire; it's a complicated matter to fire.

Early on in the planting of your church, there is always going to be a lack of adequate leaders. With that lack you will be tempted to prematurely put in places of leadership people who are not really qualified to lead.

We can guarantee—as you begin to experience church-planting momentum—there will come a hunger for staff positions and recognition among your people. A thought to consider: Instead of giving out titles such as deacon or elder early in your church's history, avoid the problems that come with naming leaders too early by describing instead of naming their ministry. Tell people what they *do*, not what they *are*. For example, we (Steve's church) have always had deacons at our church, but we have never called them that. Instead we simply call them small-group leaders. They do all the biblical things that deacons do but without the formal title. This arrangement has worked well for us for years.

Keep positional authority close to your vest for as long as you can. On the other hand, you will have to give lots of people responsibilities. When you do, you will need to keep them accountable. If you don't delegate, give things away and let people fail, they will never grow.

We don't want people to get caught up in their identities as positional leaders; rather, we intentionally downplay the significance of these positions. People who esteem titles are dangerous to themselves and the church. They become destructive—they want the position more than an identity as a servant.

There's an inverse relationship between a person's need for notoriety and their value in serving. The more someone needs recognition and the more they need other's praise, the more they are unable to handle visible positions of responsibility.

We frequently see this pattern. There are huge numbers of people who want to be on staff at churches—it's all so twisted! They scream out, "I need that position to validate me." That validation is something they can only get from Christ.

Most leaders can read that attitude in people. Listen to that—discern it in the people you consider putting on staff or taking into key volunteer roles.

Usually the people who should be recognized will not ask for it because authentic leadership lives in humility.

We have found that there is a tendency for leaders to lead well enough when we spontaneously recruit them minus a title, but as soon as we give them a title many become ineffective.

68 | Hire the right people from the beginning.

It would be nice if you could always find the perfect people for the openings you have, but it will not work that way! Every once in a while you will be blessed and actually hire a great person early on, but for the most part your initial hires will have a numbing level of frustration.

- In general, hire people who are strong in areas where you personally are weak.
- Hire what will help the church more effectively grow numerically.
- Begin to look for staff additions right from the beginning even though you have no money to pay them. It can't hurt to dream. You never know when a growth spurt is going to happen and a windfall is going to empower you to make that desired staffing addition.
- As a young church planter, I (Steve) was always looking for good staff additions. I found that we tended to find what we were looking for.
- All business people I know affirm the truth that the single most difficult thing in business is hiring the right people. The same is true in church planting and ministry.
- The right people are usually self-identifying. They come to you, and somehow it becomes clear that they

are the right ones to be on the team. This way is a lot easier than your having to go out and recruit others from scratch.

The real task is helping the people who don't belong there to leave on time. It's the displacement theory. It's removing the wrong person so that the there is space for the right person to show up and have a space to work.

The greatest differences you will have with staff will be based on certain members' opinions about what you should be doing. They will try to change your thinking, or they will try to influence the vision of the church planter by doing things their way. They are comfortable creating conflict because then they will force you to talk to them. But it's a draining process because they have a different agenda. It comes down to who's in charge and who's not. It comes down to "I'm doing this and you're not."

A few years ago we (Steve's church) had a staff member in the area of prayer who just didn't fit. It became increasingly apparent that he didn't work well in our organization because his values were so vastly different. When we started out our journey it seemed like we were a match for each other, but after a year it was apparent to a number of those who worked with him and to the fellow himself that this was a mismatched situation. For a few months he had actually been trying to change us—a losing battle, since we clearly understood what our values in prayer were and precisely why we held these values. He was too serious. He was often harsh in his dealings with people who were hurting emotionally.

One day I called him into my office and I simply gave him permission to be somewhere else in ministry. I said, "You know, this obviously isn't working out any longer. I think you would be happier ministering somewhere else where they see prayer the same way as you see it." He was greatly relieved. His face told the entire story. He looked like a load of bricks had been removed from his shoulders. He was no longer going to have to fight a battle. The possibility existed that he could go somewhere else where he was a better fit.

Within two weeks he had found another ministry that believed as he did, and he started working there. He was as happy as a clam.

69 | Create your own vision, values, mission and philosophy. Don't use anyone else's.

In another point we wrote, "Be blessed and borrow." Here we are saying seemingly the opposite. There is a time to borrow and a time to be original. When it comes to self-definition, you need to be yourself.

Listen and watch for the concepts and words of God as they come to you.

It will take some time for these demarcations to take shape—perhaps even years. At the beginning of your church plant, much of your time will be spent as a scribe logging these things for future application. Listen and watch for the concepts and words of God as they come to you.

When I (Rob) was consulting a group of pastors in the Midwest, I assigned a group to share their current vision, values and mission statements. One of the pastors came up with a rather snappy list that was very impressive. "Where did you get this?" I asked.

"I don't know," the pastor replied. "I think from someone in Chicago."

Well, he got it from me. I had written the list four years earlier. I responded that these were great ideas, but they weren't his yet. They needed to be reworded using his own language and style.

The lesson to be learned here: There's nothing wrong with borrowing bits and pieces of snappy language from here and there (as long as you are careful not to violate copyright laws), but ultimately the finished product has to come from your heart. If it comes lock, stock and barrel from someone else and bypasses your mind and heart it means precisely nothing and will not motivate anyone in your church to rally together to action.

You need to find your own way—to think through your own heart-level values. These are the ones that you discover and then shape with your own words.

70 | Be an eclectic original.

Eclecticism is important. Have lots of different interests. Get exposure to lots of influences. You need to be able to talk about a variety of things. If you can, you will attract broader-minded and better-read people. You need to be able to attract this kind of people to permanently support a church plant.

"Eclectic original" means you are creating in yourself a unique leader that hasn't existed before. You're not a replication of all the people you've ever seen. Nor are you a duplication of all the people who talk about ministry but don't live it out—just as you aren't a copy of all the people who espouse holiness but don't love the poor.

If you are a person who talks about something and does it, that becomes an attractive package. That's the type of leader people want to follow, hang out with and listen to. If you talk it, walk it.

Your goal is to be a great and fun leader who embodies quality.

Your goal is to be a great and fun leader who embodies quality. You need to have enough variety and different interests to make you an original—so that you have more to talk about than just the religious world. For example, know something about canoeing, World War II history, Teddy Roosevelt, cartoons or cooking—the things that seem like a waste of time on the surface, perhaps, but the things that make us able to be heard in the long run. If you are in a beach town, learn something about surfing. If you are near the Mexican border, learn something about Zapata and Mexican history. If are in Seattle, learn something about latte and aerospace.

Life gets really dull and boring. If you accept and act upon our encouragement to be well-read and not boring, you will thank us. Your interest in a wider spectrum of things brings texture and color when you need them the most.

71 | In your teaching and communication, don't seek to be profound or original. Plagiarize like crazy!

Don't blindly copy others' approaches without having a sense of guidance.

On the other hand, don't be so proud that you can't learn from what others are doing effectively. Take what others are doing and make it your own. A well-known preacher likes to say that the first time he repeats a quote he names the source. The second time he says, "Like someone says." The third time he says, "Like I've always said." In other words, Don't worry too much about sources. My (Steve's) take is that life moves too quickly to always be attributing the original source of every thought or idea. It's OK to aspire to cite all of your sources fully and something you obviously want to attempt with copyrighted material, but if you try to track down and attribute everything you will be fighting the illusion that there actually are new things under the sun. There is nothing new under the sun—that's biblical.

CLASSIC MISTAKES

72 | Sheep puke if they eat too much.

Don't give the whole counsel of God in one message. There must be an outward element in every church if church health is to be had. Give a tidbit of truth. Give plenty of examples about it. Illustrate it—unpack it. Make it practical. Preaching should leave people slightly satiated but not full. If you send them home full, they won't come back.

Don't just feed the sheep, but give them an opportunity to give away, to give of themselves. There is always a balance between giving and taking. If people take and take and take, they will not be in a balanced state.

There are people who can preach for 45 minutes to an hour and people don't seem ready to puke, but 99.9 percent of us (including the authors of this book) can't do that. People will just stand up and walk out in the midst of our sermon.

- Keep your messages to 30 minutes or less in length.
- Limit the topic you are going to cover. This is where preplanning messages comes in handy. If you are working on your message on Saturday night, you are always going to wander and give away too much each time.
- If you take more than half an hour, it means that you didn't do your homework adequately.

73 | Don't yell at the sheep—they won't get it.

Be gentle. Whatever you're angry at, it's not the fault of the people in your church. Spend time discovering why you're really angry. Anger usually has to do with unmet expectations.

Examine your heart. Are you really angry with God? Have you told Him? Have you had a testy discussion with Him? Does your theology allow you to do so?

Are you so frustrated that you don't think you can get past your anger? If you are convinced that you are so incensed that this is not going to disappear, then go away and discover why what is upsetting you is going on—do so in a counseling environment. Or get alone with God on a silent retreat to allow Him to speak to you.

It's easy to get frustrated and yell at the people who aren't there at your meetings. People will always disappoint you, especially early on, because there are fewer of them to whom you can spread the frustration.

After some years into my church plant, I (Steve) got to the point of being so frustrated that I couldn't come early to weekend celebrations—so I came late on purpose. I entered through the side door as the worship band was wrapping up, not long before it was time for me to speak. I became easily distracted with so many things that went wrong on a typical Sunday morning. In order to be clear minded, in the early days of the church plant, I also had to drive to church via a certain way so as to not be completely distracted by the time I arrived.

Consider doing the following to minimize the frustration levels in your life:

- Begin a journal and write down what you are mad at. Use any language needed to say what you need to say. Make sure this is private and that no one else will be able to see it.
- Commit to pray for a week or more for the individuals whom you are angry at. Allow God to change your heart.
- Invite other people to analyze how you communicate your mood in various situations. Let them give you feedback regarding how you appear.
- Take a break. Take an extended hiatus from multiweekend preaching, and have anyone else preach but you. If you have that anger spewing out of you, no matter what you say, it's all going to be tainted.
- Learn about your own natural rhythms. Know when you need to take a break and plan for it.
- Develop specific frustration-releasing hobbies. These are intentional hobbies that relate to stress release.

74 | Preach to the people who *are* there.

Every church planter has known the frustration of setting up a room for 50 people (50 who *promised* to be there!) and only 25 show up.

You are disappointed, angry and feel lied to. You are naturally focused on who's not there. You've put so much of your value on who has not shown up that you feel like a failure. It's good to get out of this habit because people will let you down over and over again. This situation will happen when you have 1,000 people in your church. You might have a Christmas event that is preceded by lots of advertising and only half as many people show up as you anticipated. It will feel like a complete waste of time.

The challenge is to preach to those 25 who did show up as though there were 5,000. These are the 25 most important people in the world because they are the 25 that Jesus has given you for right now.

It's only natural to be ticked off when you arrive only to find that a small crowd has gathered—and that after you have diligently prepared to speak all week. It's only natural to give a shallow message and then accompany that with a second subtle message that is filled with barbs and jabs at those who are missing in action.

- Abandon your expectations—give the whole thing to God.
- Select one person in the audience who you know does need to hear what you have to say. Then speak directly to him or her, but don't stare!
- Think of Jesus. How many times did He have this sort of thing happen to Him? He was let down constantly—and He is the Son of God! If it happened to the Master . . .
- Remember when this has happened to you in the past and something good came from it. Often God does unique, new things in situations like these—not necessarily in the situations that look terrific.

A Modus Operandi

75 | Plan your messages one year in advance.

You have lots of things tugging at your time and attention. By planning your messages out on a long-term basis, you will have one less item to have to think about from week to week.

Doing messages in series format is a great idea, but how do you start? You prepackage something several months in advance. You will likely ask, *How in the world am I going to get enough time to do that?*

- **Step one**: Sit down with a team of trusted people and discuss all of the issues, values and biblical truths that need to be discussed over the next year.
- **Step two**: Search out quality messages from good communicators on the same or similar topics.
- **Step three**: Work what you find into an initial schedule over the next year, and add individual messages to fill in between various series of lessons.
- **Step four**: Purchase the series necessary.
- **Step five**: Isolate yourself and prepare the messages. Determine what information, data and illustrations you will need to complete the messages.
- **Step six**: Set up a review process with your team as a monthly process to see how it's going and where it's going.

During that first attempt at planning your message, plan for six months ahead. The second time you do this routine get a one-year cycle on paper. When you are finished with the process, you should be working on messages that you will deliver a year away for this same month.

76 | *Never* cancel an event.

There is a lot of chaos in the early days of a church plant. People who promise to show up or to lead this or that fall through at the last minute. This may sound counter to the message of excellence, counter to your intuition, but it pans out in the long run: *Never cancel an event.* There will repeatedly be temptations to cancel events due to low attendance, weather conditions or a myriad of other excuses, but don't give in to the temptation. Don't let anger and frustration get the best of you.

**When you say you
personally will be there or
your church says it will be there,
then be there.**

When your church is small, you don't cancel stuff. Likewise, when you are big, you don't cancel stuff. When you say you personally will be there or your church says it will be there, then be there. Once you've communicated an event, never call it off.

Many times we have been tempted to cancel events but never gave in to that desire. We always ended up following through only to discover that plenty of people showed up. Literally every time we went forward with an event and didn't give in to the desire to cancel, we found the number of people in attendance made the event to be absolutely worthwhile. Both of us have Christmas Eve stories in which we considered canceling services due to snowy weather, but we persevered. In the end the events were wonderful. Lots of people came. Stories abounded about how difficult it was to get to the facility. All of those stories made the evening even more special.

77 | A great weekend gathering experience is critical. This is the time when you publicly display your congregation's soul.

Find your place—the balance in your fellowship's profile. It's the face you present to the city.

Atmosphere architects plan things from the beginning. You are creating an environment to which people will want to return. It's a place where people find grace and peace. When you are starting out, those are high aspirations. You'll build a group of habits that you won't break. You will be building a group of assumptions that people will have about your church. This will make up your liturgy. These are important times.

Worship needs to be transcendent. Pray for God's presence. Have a dream in mind. Have you been to a church and really loved what you saw? Did you look at the hearts of the people? Are you learning how to pray as they prayed? Be able to visualize what you saw and reproduce it at your location.

Your people need to get a sense of God's presence each time they come to church. They have big problems, and they need to meet up with Big God every time they come to a weekend celebration at your church plant.

- Seek quality, not perfectionism. In our day of seeker-targeted churches, it is increasingly common for churches not to know how to discern the difference between quality and perfectionism. You know you have fallen into perfectionism when nerves are frayed, feelings are being hurt, the celebration is no longer fun, and there is more of an emphasis on performing the show than on looking for God's presence in your meetings.

- *Transformations* occur during celebration times. People being in the presence of God causes something life changing to happen. People are changed when worshiping with one another—something happens as we sing songs to God together. We are bonded together. We hear God together. We begin to see what we can become when we are gathered together. We can begin to believe big things when we are together—things that are impossible to believe when we are alone. We need to work and pray to that end. *Cohesion* also happens during these times.

This is where vision is released. The gifts of teaching and leadership are most clearly expressed at these times. This is where the city gets an opportunity to participate in the life of your community and be transcendent together with you. This is the primary place where you want to invest yourself as the atmosphere architect. If this works, then everything else pivots off of it. This is key.

78 | Begin to delegate now.

Look for people who have different gifts than the ones you have—let them do the work you ask and honor them for their faithfulness. Thank them—learn the fine art of regularly, continually thanking people in ways that make sense to them. There are lots of ways to thank people.

From the first planning meeting, delegation is the name of the game. From then on, it needs to grow through the power of the people. It's the first tool to teach your leaders in your ways. If you aren't also requiring them to delegate, you are crippling them. If you are requiring them to delegate, then you are drawing out the best in them. You are releasing the best of the gifts in the community. You are activating the community. You are reducing the stress on any one person, especially yourself.

You need to build in delegation as an organizational habit.

Five steps to conveying a new behavior:

1. Do it alone.
2. Do it with someone watching you do it.
3. Do it with someone helping you do it.
4. The other person does it while you watch them.
5. The other person does it with someone else watching them do it.

When the church planter gives away duties and responsibilities he or she will go through stress—mostly caused by timing. When do you delegate?

There is a difference between delegation and abdication. This is always a concern for church planters. Delegation is giving someone the responsibility and the authority to accomplish a job while they remain accountable to someone else. Abdication abandons the final accountability.

There are some aspects of ministry that you can't and shouldn't give away. On the other hand, there are some that need to definitely be given away to others early on. The idea is to do it in a healthy way.

How do you maintain delegation?

- *It's valuable to check up weekly on all the people to whom you have delegated.* Do you maintain consistent regular accountability with each person individually? Do you know what they are achieving or not achieving? Do you know if they are being successful or not? Are the expectations for each person written and are they reviewed? Have they given you feedback—negative or positive—regarding how they feel about their work? If so, did you listen? What influence will their feelings have on how they perform?

- So much is going on and coming at you, you often don't hear, "I hate this." If you do get that sort of feedback, you need to know what to do about it.

- As the senior leader, your job is to bring encouragement to the team by reminding them of the big picture they are all working toward. Help them to see how their contribution is helping to extend the kingdom of God.

- Brag on your volunteers. Repeat stories of how people were touched by their ministry.

- Help your team members find the areas to serve that best suit them. Give lots of praise.

- Correct behavior that needs correcting, but don't ever attack a person. Respect his or her time and investment in this exciting church plant.

79 | Build a first-class worship experience.

Spend the money that is available and then some. People will judge you and even brand you on the basis of your sound. "That's the church with a great band!"

Aspire to be distinct. It's not necessarily good to try to be like everyone else or even anyone else that you've heard or seen before. It's good to just be like you are.

- **Be in touch *vertically*.** Be cognizant of what God is doing in your midst. If you lack discernment in this area, pray and God will make you sensitive to His Spirit's moving. It isn't a spooky or bizarre thing, but a

> Be cognizant of what God is doing in your midst.

natural matter of being aware of the moving of the Holy Spirit in a place during worship.
- **Be in touch *horizontally*.** Be aware of the people dynamics in the room. Are they getting tired? Are they getting bored? Is it time to quit doing worship even though you have two more songs on the agenda? It is better to go a little shorter than to bore people who are for some reason not into worship that day.

Remember the quote from G. K. Chesterton, "Anything worth doing is worth doing poorly."[5] Don't demand perfection starting out of the gates. On the other hand, there is a need for a measure of excellence—raising the bar to where you are going to be.

Here are several points to remember:

- **You are mostly singing to God, not to man.** Choose songs that are written in the first-person voice, like the Psalms, or have a vertical focus rather than a horizontal one. Check out the Passion CDs, produced by Louie Giglio, for some new inspiration.[6] Many bands are coming out with great worship CDs, band such as Third Day, Delirious and Sonic Flood. Check out the Vineyard UK, Matt Redman and Kate Miner, to name a few. "Lord I Lift Your Name on High" and "We Are Gathered in This Place to Worship You" focus on the Lord. You are going to love God actively as you sing. This gets you in touch with God.

- **It's easier to find skilled musicians and then teach them how to worship than the reverse.** We have even allowed, on occasion, not-yet-Christians to play in our worship bands. They inevitably become believers. Probably the most frustrating approach to worship leading is taking someone with no musical background and starting from scratch. Musically inclined people will find it very difficult to worship in a setting like that. You may appreciate the effort the worship leader is putting out, but anyone with musical ability will notice that this person is unskilled.

- **Don't let your worship band become too large.** I've seen small churches with very large worship bands—sometimes the bands were a fourth of the entire church! It looks odd, and it's simply unnecessary. Simplicity is best—especially when you are starting out.

- **Make sure the people who are visible on the worship team represent the racial diversity of your entire church.** Minorities will notice and be appreciative of the inclusion of some of their own in your band as well as some of their sound in the worship flavor.

80 | Read to lead.

Both of us early on in our Christian lives have been encouraged to read as much and as broadly as possible.[7] We are glad we received that counsel when we started out. The reasons are many.

- Reading increases your well-roundedness—it makes you a much more interesting conversationalist. As we have already noted, if you hope to reach a more sophisticated population, you will need to be able to converse with them.
- Reading gives you consistent sources to draw from when your public speaking gets dry or frustrating.

> **Reading is the ultimate way to develop yourself and get insight on becoming the best leader you can be.**

- Reading is very attractive to big thinkers and other highly skilled leaders.
- Reading helps you develop insight and effective strategic planning.
- Reading breeds wisdom. Studying the works of great thinkers and people who lived godly lives will imbue your life with wisdom.
- Reading will make you a better exegete of your city and of your Bible.

Reading is the ultimate way to develop yourself and get insight on becoming the best leader you can be. Read in areas where you are going to need to grow. For example, pick up a basic text on marketing and merchandising. Even if you don't need this kind of knowledge, you will need to be able to communicate with others who are conversant in those areas.

- You need to read many crucial books that help you define yourself, your target, your mission and your style.
- Make reading part of your daily discipline.
- Read quickly—learn to scan for information. Take a speed-reading class at your local community college or university. It will be well worth the investment of time and money.
- Read significant magazines that will keep you abreast of current events and stories that are worth following, such as *Time*, *The Economist*, *Utne Reader*, *Wired*, *Christianity Today*, *Charisma*, *Fast Company* and *Rolling Stone*. In addition I (Steve) read *USA Today* every day. Some e-zines that are worth reading are regeneration.org, ooze.com and slate.com.

81 | Win the kids and you will win the parents. Kids' church isn't a baby-sitting service. You'll pay if you think that way.

It is a standard misconception among church planters that you spend all your money on adults and that you spend the minimum amount possible on children. The danger is in treating children's church like it's a babysitting service. It seems easy to provide the children care that is just good enough to survive. Many such decisions are made because it seems that when resources are at a premium, children are not a good investment. Church planters tend to view child care this way: Parents will not return if there is not some kind of care for their children.

One of the problems with that view is that it makes them children, not Christians or followers. They are essentially not part of the church—they are something that you need to deal with in order to have church.

The reality is that children matter to God! Look at Jesus. He put children at the center and said they are people with the most clout! Embrace children as full-fledged followers of Jesus Christ. They already can and do hear God. They already can and will serve and give to the Kingdom. They have significant influence as people who already have the ear of their parents.

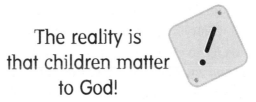

The reality is that children matter to God!

Parents ask their children two questions when they get to the car after church: "Did you have fun?" and "Did you learn anything?" If you can pass the test on those two accounts, you will pass the test with the parents. It's about that simple.

- Gather a group of parents—particularly moms—and have a meeting during which they present their dream children's church using your current facility. Go into significant detail about their wish list. What color should the paint be? What sorts of cribs? Which manufacturer?
- Spend time, if you can, with an interior designer. He or she may be able to help you design something with a more spacious feel despite the limitations of your facility.
- Go for light and bright. It's amazing what a couple of cans of paint and a couple of your friends can accomplish.
- Plan on spending a considerable amount of time thanking and praising anyone who contributes to the children's church. They are your heroes!

- As soon as you can, pay someone to cover your nursery. The crib area is the most crucial and scary to young moms. If you have a paid nursery worker there each week, along with your volunteers, you will build safety and security for moms and babies alike.

- You need to be training your people that they should not be involved in more than two activities at church. And children's church should count for two of those things, because in a new church there will be a significant amount of activity involved in setting up and tearing down each Sunday. It will be a consuming activity.

- Preplan within the first 12 months a vacation for every volunteer. This does a lot for morale. It forces you to understand that burnout will happen to every volunteer no matter what he or she says. It forces you to prearrange who will fill in when the regulars are on vacation. This step communicates respect and admiration for the work done with children. Volunteers will thank you for your leadership and professionalism when they return from vacation.

- Use a well-known national curriculum. Gospel Light, David C. Cook and Faith Weaver by Group Inc. are all great resources. They have every possible graphic already done. Just as you want to use someone else's messages when you begin your church, you also want to use someone else's children's church material.

- Remember, children will destroy their physical environment—twice as fast as adults. Expect that regularly you will have to change the carpet, repaint, fix hardware and repair countertops. If you are setting up and putting away in someone else's building, realize that things are going to break on a regular basis there, too. You will need to have a crew designated to make repairs in your rented facility. You'll clean up and mend your children's church as if you were living in a fraternity house.

- Make sure that the children's church volunteers have the opportunity and the encouragement to do outreach. They have to be filled with Jesus' passion for the lost. If they aren't doing it, they can't communicate it to the children.

- Make sure every volunteer goes through a background screening no matter how close a friend he or she is. This screening should include criminal record information and any sexual improprieties.

- Have a weekend of training for anyone who goes into the classroom—enunciate your philosophy of ministry, goals and values. Include team-building exercises to help everyone get to know each other better. And don't forget to make it fun!

- Have a policeman in the children's area before and after the offering. This is very productive. It gives the parents a great sense of security and allows the children to interact with the policeman and have a great experience.

82 | To be profound is better than to be cute.

In your initial gathering, don't be cute—be profound. We notice cute all over the place when we see new churches attempting to gather their first crowd. We can't even remember the number of cutesy mailers we've received inviting us to come to the opening service of a new church in town. After a short time they all look alike. They all claim to be "not like your mom and dad's church." Our moms and dads didn't go to church, so we don't even know what they are talking about!

Typical unchurched, postmodern people aren't looking for cute. In fact, they are cute averse. Cute is a big turnoff. It's all too slick. Authenticity versus excellence is an important question to raise.

One of the church planters that I (Steve) coach started his church by using a series of mass mailing flyers that went out to tens of thousands of people in his community. He did a high quality job on all of the flyers. They were multi-colored and very attractive. He did a new mailer each quarter announcing his new teaching series in his attempt to raise awareness of his new church.

Typical unchurched, postmodern people aren't looking for cute.

While there was nothing wrong with his mailers, my counsel to him was to step away from the cute approach and to become profound in his outreach to the community. Some time ago he and I began to go door to door collecting food in a simple way—armed with just a squeaky wheelbarrow. To people in the upscale neighborhood near his church plant come to the door we announce that we are collecting food for a party for single moms. After collecting food for a few days we had enough to throw a party for the needy moms in a certain neighborhood that his church is focusing on in their outreaches.

The good news is that his church is now growing at rate that is faster than when he was using the slick mailers.

Cute warning signs. If you see these, be concerned.
- Having sugary-sweet people in positions of authority is really a bad deal.

- Trying to do what everyone else is doing.
- Trying to be big when you are little.

Profound things you can do:
- Serious doesn't necessarily mean that it's over the top for a Sunday newcomer.
- Advertising by attraction rather than by promotion.
- Don't overpromote your church's name—promote the name of Christ and the cause of the Kingdom. That sort of behavior will cause people to remember both Christ and your church in the end.
- Involve people in service. Meet the needs of someone. Do what Jesus did—that generally works!

83 | Learn to tell your story—well!

- Have a 3-minute version of your vision story.
- Have a 5-minute version.
- Have a 15-minute version.

Learn to smile big when you are telling your story. Be enthusiastic, not fake.

Picture each person as someone God may be giving you as a gift. If they aren't your gift, they are someone else's. Your job is to direct that gift to where he or she belongs.

You aren't selling something. You are making people aware of the greatest thing that might happen in their lifetimes—their involvement in your church plant.

I (Steve) can tell you that during the past 20 years I've had many people come up to me and, while choking down tears, say, "You know, I've had a great life, but being involved with this church has been the single most life-changing experience I've been through." You will have people tell you the same thing! Remember this when you go out to tell your story. Each time you sit down to communicate your vision—whatever version it may be, even if it's the 3-minute one—realize that you are doing something that may well be the most significant thing that the person will experience in his or her lifetime. That will put a new spin on your storytelling.

Here is how to tell a great vision story:

- Practice telling your story when you are alone. Then practice telling it to a few friends. First work at getting it down to three minutes. Think of the 5-minute and 15-minute versions as luxuries. Get a stopwatch. We really mean that many minutes. As with any sort of public speaking, you will be forced not to go over the time limit, which means you will have to cut out certain points that don't fit.

 **Remember that your story is a part of God's story.**

- Find someone who is a veteran storyteller and ask him or her how they tell stories. Hopefully that person will be a church planter. If you can't find anyone, contact me (Steve) and I will give you some pointers that fit your specific situation.
- Create outlines for all three versions of your vision talk and keep them on your Palm Pilot.
- Make sure you tell your vision from the perspective of how it's going to benefit the hearer rather than how it will benefit you or the organization.

- When you tell your story, allow the hearer to comment on it honestly.
- If your story doesn't have pop and zing to it, adjust it until it does. Ask your listener if it is interesting. If it isn't, ask him or her what you can add so that it will pop and zing.
- Remember that your story is a part of God's story. He is doing big stuff through you and your church plant, and He wants to do big stuff through the people He brings to you.

84 | Pay big-time attention to newcomers.

If you do this, the already-gathered, already believers will no doubt complain that they are not receiving adequate attention. "What about us? Are we chopped liver or what?" they will no doubt ask. Such questions are only natural. You need to explain to the already-gathered people that these newcomers are the way forward for the fellowship as a whole. Some will not understand and will make it evident that perhaps they are not destined to be long-term participants in your new venture.

In showing attention to newcomers, we recommend a few simple steps that will translate to them as care and concern.

- As we have already noted, a personal handwritten letter from the senior leader, sent out on Sunday night.
- A brief call on Wednesday to follow up on the letter (no more than two-to-three minutes long). Say something like this: "I'm so glad you were able to be with us. I'd love to get together with you at some point in the near future to answer any questions you have about our church." We recommend you call during the day when

you are likely to get an answering machine. The idea
here is to leave a message, not to bother people.

- When you make the telephone call, invite the newcomer out for a piece of pie. Pie is a friendly food. (By the
way, for the record, the most unfriendly food to eat
with strangers is raw onions.) At this encounter, give
them a brief chance to interact with you regarding your
fellowship. I've found that a high percentage of those
who come out for pie stay around the church for an
extended period—at least partly because they've been
shown a little personal attention.

- Steer them toward your newcomers' class or classes
that you have set up to explain the whats and whys of
your church plant. You could also direct newcomers to
an Alpha class if you offer one.

85 | Great worship and great music.

This doesn't need to be complex. In fact, the simpler the better.
The goal is to do what it takes to usher in Big God's presence
when you gather together for your Sunday celebrations.

This is an area that will be constantly scrutinized and regularly improved. Your team needs to understand that you aren't
striving to get something decent and then leave it that way for
years. Constant improvement is a proper heart attitude toward
all the things that are being improved in the church.

With worship, the idea is to go where your heart is leading
you—be honest and go there. The worship you do in your first
six months is not going to be much like the worship you do in
year three. Even though people may judge you, things are in flux.
This isn't like the previous church where people have been
before—and that is a good thing.

Here is how you can have great worship (some points are repeated from earlier in this book, but they are worth pondering again):

- Don't put up with bad musicians. You may be desperate, but you aren't that desperate. If necessary, go with fewer musicians. A simpler great sound is more desirable than something that is lower in quality.
- Have a full run-through of your worship set on a separate day other than your worship time. This will take a significant amount of time—perhaps another reason that the person in charge of your worship ought to be paid a salary.
- You will always be advertising and looking for new musicians. You can't have enough skilled worship-team members. Musicians burn out, too. The need is especially true for your dream of going to two services.
- Don't scrimp on musical equipment and sound reinforcement. Great musicians will be embarrassed if you don't have adequate equipment for them to use. If you don't take care, you could eventually lose your best musicians.

86 | Great atmosphere.

Do people want to stick around when your services are over, or do they quickly leave? In the final analysis, it's all about atmosphere. Do you have a buzz about your place or don't you? This is the difference between an OK gathering time and seeing something special going on with your new church.

- It's a prayer thing. If you are not seeing a buzz happening, then you need to pray. It's one of the barometers that you can measure to see if God is up to something or not. It begins with prayer.
- You can't force an atmosphere to happen. You have to let it unfold. The harder you try to create an atmosphere, the more elusive it becomes. It's like swimming toward a beach ball in the ocean; the harder you swim toward it the further away it gets.
- Catching the vibe isn't something that you can program.
- One of the profound ways to develop atmosphere is to sing great songs. There's no excuse for not singing platinum-level songs. Simply refuse to sing bad ones. There are enough awesome songs available that you should never have to sing anything but a great one.

When establishing a good atmosphere, you want to avoid these mood breakers:

- Talking too much. Either talk or sing worship songs, but don't try to do both. The only time you need to talk is when you've planned to talk.
- Delay between songs. There needs to be a flow from song to song. Practice what notes will be played between songs.
- When the worship leader is in performance mode instead of worship mode, he or she will get in the way of others worshiping.
- When the worship band is not worshiping, the people will not worship.
- Children in the worship service. If you manage children in the service well, it can add to the service (this rarely

happens), but a disturbance by a child can detract from a service (this is common).

87 | Great communication.

You flavor all of your communication based on who you are. You have to know who you are to do that. The messages do not necessarily just communicate biblical truth but also what it's like with your group to be a disciple. It's like cooking a meal. It's the experience of eating. It's going to the most wonderful place in the world for Thanksgiving. Smells fill the air. There's the layout of the food. People are renewing old friendships. There's lots of conversation. Prayer is just the right thing said. When it comes time to leave, people wish they didn't have to go and start Christmas shopping the next day.

So when we talk about communication, we come from that perspective. It's not a matter of whether you are going to feed your friends or not, but what kind of silverware you are going to use. It's not asking whether you are going to serve food or whether you care, but whether what you have to offer matches what they need.

When talking about messages, for example, what we want to think about is the aroma. How have you cooked the turkey this year? What spices have you used? How have you made sure that the different elements of the meal will all come out hot at the same time?

Messages: How are you connecting to the real world? What's on the front page of the newspaper today? How are you going to use that? It has to have an aroma. Most of the time at most churches when it comes to the message you receive, you get an overcooked piece of chicken with no spices in it at all.

A lot of diction and speech are connected with the presentation of the words that are chosen. I (Steve) had to slow down my speaking speed in order to become more effective. I had to get my teeth reworked including getting braces in order to be clearly understood. Good communication is more than knowing your Bible, having a big smile and wanting to tell someone. I had to go in for speech lessons.

Are you willing to change when things that need to be changed are pointed out to you?

The primary skill in this area is the need for courage once you have found a coach who can speak into your life. Are you willing to change when things that need to be changed are pointed out to you?

88 | Visual Communications: PowerPoint—LCD projector with remote.

When you walk into your family Thanksgiving gathering, there are sights that are appropriate and that go with the holiday. So it is with a celebration. The kingdom of God is a party. What is it that makes for a great Thanksgiving? People who come who are just happy to see you and whom you are happy to see. The intangibles are what you pick up on in the first two minutes. What are the details? As far as the party goes, it is primarily a feminine skill. Make sure you are including women in the preparations.

Music must communicate. We're talking about the volume as well as the genre. It all comes together to make up the complete package.

Fill in the blank outlines. For many this type of interaction is helpful—for others it's too linear. It helps draw people into the party. But at some Thanksgiving parties it would simply not fit. Having a place card with what is going to be served—this would make a lot of sense if you had a group of people over the age of 40 who are upper middle class and above. You need to do what makes the most sense for the group of people that God has given to you.

Be uniquely eclectic—gather information from all sorts of sources:

- Photos and artwork from your people make great slide shows to go with a message or to provoke thought and prayer.
- Have an artist create something like a painting for one of your messages or, more radical still, during one of your services.
- Art and photos from the Web are also great slide shows.
- Magazines.
- Websites.
- TV—use everything from commercials to *The West Wing*! Make sure you know what Oprah is doing. She has more influence on the spirituality of our country than most churches.
- Movies like *Ice Ace*. This film is about how one person can change the world, or how a baby brings enemies together. Try Hollywoodjesus.com for a Christian perspective on current films.
- Books—especially those being read by the masses, such as the Harry Potter series, Dr. Phil or Tolkien.

89 | Clarify your job description.

Our intent is to make sure that you require of yourself the same 40 hours of work per week that everybody else in your church puts in, if not more. You need a schedule of when you get up in the morning and when you go to bed, just like everybody else.

Do servant-evangelism projects between appointments to get into the community.

Get up early enough to have breakfast meetings with people—that is a prime time for telling your story. Lunch is another good time. Afternoon coffee is a valuable time as well.

- Do servant-evangelism projects between appointments to get into the community. Before long many people will know who you are.
- Pray around your neighborhood and the community you are seeking to impact. Get some friends to go with you, and then get them to prayer walk around malls, buildings, schools, etc. Claim the land!
- Make sure you leave the house every morning—no later than 9:00.
- We encourage you to get an office outside of your house—no matter how cheap it is. You need to leave your family to themselves and go off to work like everyone else in your community. This is the key to your mental health and that of your family. This move will keep your kids from hating what you are doing.
- During the evenings, lead and model small-group lead-

ership as you raise up leaders.
- Don't stay up late. Go to bed early if you can, so you can get up early in the morning.
- How much time per week should you expect to spend on routine busywork? Manage volunteers to do this—aggressively limit doing that sort of thing to 25 percent of your time.

The priorities are what need to be focused upon. Those are:

- gathering,
- training small-group leaders,
- defining and honing the vision and
- assimilating newcomers into your group.

Your job description is a moving target that will be adjusted as you surge forward. Every church planter struggles with how best to use his time. See the section in the appendix about progressive job descriptions (see p. 193).

Pray for a good—make that a great—assistant who has strong administrative and relational skills.

90 | A church with fewer than 200 people is struggling.

With fewer than 200 people, a church will need to fight just to stay alive. With fewer than that number of people, you will not have hit your stride. It is inevitable that your attention will be focused upon simply trying to maintain the basics of church survival. With fewer than 200 people, a church is at the stage of just hanging in there. Almost everything that goes on is a struggle to pull off each week. For example, there aren't enough teens to have a dynamic youth group. A children's program is a challenge to pull off because of a lack of staff and volunteers. The pastor is overworked because it seems that he does everything in the church.

There's no shame in having fewer than 200 in weekend attendance. Our suggestion, however, is that you stay at that point for as short a time as possible. Churches become toxic when they are chronically overworked. A group larger than 200 people develops enough leaders and enough resources so that everyone gets a chance to get a break. Without this break, burnout is automatic. Whether people tell you they are burning out or not, they still are. Then one day, they just leave and move on to another church because they can't handle the pressure any longer. Everybody needs a break.

 **There's no shame in having fewer than 200 in weekend attendance.**

When you grow past 200, you give the scaffolding people the invisible opportunity to leave because you don't need them to work any longer. As more successful people begin to join your ranks, the scaffolding people will be less inclined to stay. When you grow past 200, you will begin to attract successful people because you will begin to look successful. Successful people will begin to seek you out as a destination place.

What do you do if you consistently have less than 200 in weekend worship for years on end and you have the toxic situation that we've described above? Consider strongly closing your church and restarting it again. Change the name. Reexamine your vision, your assumptions, your priorities, your values. Let the thing lie fallow for six months to a year before you think of taking it up again. In the meantime, get an outside job. It will be good for your sanity to get that break. You probably will think, *What about the people—won't they scatter?* For sure, some will. Encourage them to go to other local churches during the down time. When you restart, invite them, but don't you dare see them as the core upon which you will build this new work. To do that would be to resurrect that old, sick thing that you were trying to lay down all along.

91 | Begin with two services.

Of the more than 100 points in this book, this is 1 of the top 5 that we encourage church planters to adopt. We know what you are thinking: *Two services to begin with—that's crazy!* Two services are counterintuitive, but there are many good reasons for going to two services when you go public.

- It will give you a chance to practice your message by giving it twice. It always comes out better the second time. Also, you will be required to limit what you say— something that is always a good thing.
- It creates an atmosphere—a sense of expectancy. The attitude will spread—*Wow, something great is happening here. We can't even get all of our people in here at one time.*
- It will allow you to make sure you always have room for the new people so that they have enough room to come and feel expected and welcomed.
- It will give your workers (children's church, ushers, greeters, parking lot people, etc.) a chance to go to church. They can work at one service and attend a second.

- It will break up the we-four-and-no-more mentality that so typically prevails and keeps newcomers away.
- It causes excitement when your people realize *Wow, we are large enough that we can't all meet in the same place at the same time!*
- It will allow you to take up less space in a smaller building and save you rent.
- It creates an incredible group of assumptions that come with the starting of two services—almost too many to verbalize. If you were to verbalize them, it would come off as arrogant perhaps. It is enough to say, "We are just making room for lots of people who are making their way here!"
- It's a signal to the community: We'll make room for you.

Some church planters think that they barely have the resources to pull off one service, much less two. But what we've found is that when you lay it out there and go for the two-service project, people always show up. The workers that are needed somehow come to the forefront. It is worth the risk—always.

Communicate to your people: "We intend to make a difference. Our dream for this is not small. If you are ready for a wild ride, hitch your wagon to us."

92 | Work in a nonchurch environment until the church grows larger. Work even if you don't need the extra income.

You desperately need to get into the community. You need to work no matter what your financial backing looks like. We encourage you to work outside the church until your plant reaches 200 in weekend attendance. This is to make a number of statements. The most important ones are:

- You are not trying to avoid working in the marketplace. There is nothing to avoid. That's where all the people are that you would be inviting to your church. You want to affirm that the efforts of every single one of your people who spends long hours in the workforce are of great value. You want to show them the kindnesses of the church at work in the marketplace.
- You destroy the sacred-secular conflict. By that we mean the natural inclination of most already-converted people who think that working in the church is more valuable than working in the marketplace—that it's more valued by God. Take it from two people who have spent a long time working in churches—that just isn't true. You and your people need to be out in the community.
- You continue to send the message that you aren't trying to live off of other people—that you are trying to pay your own way. Be sure to give substantially from the money you earn outside the church to the church. Great leaders are always one of the top givers in their church.
- It requires you not to be available and allows for your congregation to work out their issues on their own on occasion. Taking an outside job creates an understanding in the church that you aren't there as their free therapist. It also creates an environment in which really emotionally sick people won't have you to lean on all the time, so they will find someone else.
- It causes you to interact with the people in the marketplace—many of whom are looking for a new church to plug into. Best of all, they get to see you functioning in the role of a "normal" person outside the rank of

pastor—when they see you in church, they may have expectations and spooky baggage that they may be carrying around from previous times in their life.

93 | Know what your target's minimums and maximums are.

Our encouragement here is to know what your target people like and dislike. This is so that when you are developing video presentations, drama or experiential worship, you will know what will be attractive to your people and what will be repulsive. How conservative are they? How liberal are they? How politically aware are they? What minimum expectations do they have as far as technology, humor, seriousness, playfulness and warm fuzzies go? It's a matter of learning propriety levels and seeing how far your people will go—what they will put up with without being offended by a particular message of the gospel.

Some examples:

- What could you get away with in Redmond, Washington, home of Microsoft? Since everyone there knows about PowerPoint, you will have to do some pretty snappy presentations to make the passing grade in that city.
- If you are in Johnson City, Tennessee, PowerPoint and top-10 lists may very well make the locals just plain annoyed.
- In Los Angeles, you will have to be very culturally aware; you will have to be very aware of stereotypes; you will have to be very politically correct in whatever you do.
- If you are in Cincinnati, you want to be sensitive to Catholics in general, since 70 percent of the city is from a Roman Catholic background, and though they don't necessarily attend a Catholic church, they still revere

the Catholic name. Many of them intend for church to
be church. When they go to church, they intend to have
a church experience.

94 | You can start with the crowd and move to the core, or build from the core to the crowd.

All churches start either one way or the other—from small to
large or from large to small. Starting with the crowd and moving to the core is fun for your ego. However, when you do it
that way, you have no actual church, only a crowd after the initial wave of people come. On the other hand, starting from the
core and moving to the crowd is hard on the ego and it is slow
going.

We aren't endorsing either approach as being the superior
way to go. A large percentage of churches that we are starting are
going to start by developing the core first. Please don't consider
this a problem or a negative to the future of your church at all.
Some powerful churches have been launched with this approach.
The Vineyard in Cincinnati started with just five people!

95 | Don't start doing significant pastoral care until your church has attained critical mass.

This is one of the most common causes for loss of momentum—
of stopping growth. To begin to behave as a pastoral care expert
before your church reaches the 200 barrier will almost invariably
stop its growth. We recommend that even after your church has
attained critical mass (see glossary), you still don't do pastoral
care. That's not your job. That's the job of others you will hire
and the role of small-group leaders.

Even after you've reached that point in your growth, you as the senior leader will not be caring for the counseling needs of the flock—someone else whom you have brought on for that specific purpose will function in that role.

Your job is to care for the caregivers or small-group leaders. In the same way that you aren't going to pastor the city—you are going to pastor the people who pastor the city—so also, your job isn't to care for everyone. Your job is to train the caregivers. Attempting to take care of everyone yourself is an enormous waste of time—it keeps the people who should be doing it from doing it! Those who need the practice are prevented from getting the opportunity they need to try out and develop their ministry gifts.

Too much caring for people is a top-10 time waster for church planters.

Allow your small groups to serve as your main vehicle for pastoral care from early on. In addition, do stand-up pastoral care—that is, after meetings talk with people while literally standing up. That ensures that the counseling encounters last no more than 5 to 10 minutes. Sitting down ensures that your meeting will last half an hour or more.

96 | Learn the seven deadly sins of church leadership.

In no particular order here's how they go:

- **Fretting about what is not happening.** This is the most deadly—without a doubt, it is number one on this list. Worrying about things that are out of your control. It wastes energy, it focuses on the negative, it makes you useless when you talk to people (it makes you fake that the Kingdom is a positive thing when you feel differently, for example). This includes the con-

Top 10 Time Wasters for Church Planters

1. **Lack of a written daily plan.**
2. **Lack of deadlines.** You have to give yourself some deadlines or you will just wander.
3. **Depression.** It comes from being alone too much. Being with people on Sundays only isn't going to get it done.
4. **Pity parties.**
5. **Overly needy people.** You are not gifted or skilled to help these people beyond the application of an emotional bandage, so don't try to function as something you're not.
6. **Computers and new technology.** These can be a great help, but they can also be tremendous time wasters. These can sap hours out of your life.
7. **TV.** Enough said.
8. **Busywork.** Paperwork and other minutiae that doesn't make any difference in your forward progress.
9. **Worrying about the past.** Concern about what other people think about you, what people from school think about you and how you are being perceived by the denomination.
10. **Worrying about the future.** Concern over what may or may not be happening and if you will succeed or not. This can absorb unlimited amounts of energy.

stant nitpicking of details, from how someone is singing off-key to how the carpet is dirty. This can mount up to the point that it becomes insufferable and paralyzing.

· **Misunderstanding your community.** If there is a mismatch between you and your community, your group will never take off. This emanates from failing to be with the people of the community and knowing what they are like. This stems from a lack of research on the people group in advance of going—and failing to commit to being with them.

- **Unwillingness to meet confrontation head-on.** It seems that when you get going in church planting everyone is an expert on the subject. You will have to draw lines of demarcation. People will leave your church—it's just the way it is.
- **Jumping into planting before you have acquired the DNA to reproduce.** You will simply fail to build a foundation. Therefore, whatever you build will become top-heavy and will fall in upon itself. You will have a stillbirth.

It's superimportant that you have had adequate time to catch the norm of someone who has successfully done what you are hoping to do—even if it's a very different style. We have found that what you have had modeled to you is what you will produce. If you have been raised around churches that grow to 100 and then stop growing, you will in all likelihood produce churches exactly like that. On the other hand, if you have had an internship at a church of 5,000, where systems are emphasized and where the work of the ministry is done through a system of volunteers, you are much more likely to produce a church similar to that.

Take advantage of the opportunity to take an internship at a large, growing, dynamic church if the opportunity presents itself.

- **Not having a schedule.** That is, not forcing yourself to stay on task. There is a major difference between being a self-starter and having a job description and sticking to it.
- **Failing to make gathering your number one priority.**

- **Failing to take the long view.** You will end up hyper-analyzing short-term things that don't have an impact on long-term matters.

97 | Define yourself.

How have you come to the place where you are in your thinking, your philosophy and your priorities? Typically, all of these areas have been formed by influential leaders at places where you have been previously. You consider these leaders/mentors/models who have given you insight into the world of ministry to be highly effective. Unfortunately, none of the people who come to your church know these people, nor do they care. What they care about is that you are on the leading edge regarding what God is up to in your city.

Here are some questions that will help you begin the dialogue:

- What do you think a disciple is?
- What kind of church is going to be effective at reaching your community in 10 years?
- Who do you need to become in order to lead your church five years from now?
- What's the most important spiritual need in your life right now?
- Are there new models and new styles that need to be involved to help you evolve?

98 | Design your meetings.

There are premeditated elements that comprise all effective meetings. There are feelings and experiences that each person will take away with them from a meeting. You can't demand that they will experience something, like a robot, but you can create an environment that leads directly to experiencing the presence of God. We call it atmosphere architecture. It is taking into account every detail that goes into making up your gathering times.

Think things through in detail from beginning to end—from before they drive up until they drive away from your meeting. There's a sense of expectation. There's a sense of joyfulness. There's a conviction of Big God's presence. There's a feeling of breakthrough. There's an experience of healing. These are all things that you would not only pray through but also plan for

Our prayer is that the newcomer would experience a sense of coming home— of being truly wanted.

so that others would experience them when they come to your meetings. That impacts your choice of songs. That has to do with how you communicate verbally. That has to do with the use of greenery and other props, musicians, the kinds of sound systems and the sorts of people who meet them when they walk in the door. It has to do with the sorts of stories you tell when you are giving the message. I (Steve) know that when I am speaking at a church and I tell a servant-evangelism story, I can literally change the atmosphere in the room. You too can change the atmosphere when you tell a compelling story.

A church plant has a lot more flexibility than an existing church. With rental space and enough greenery, you can turn your facility into the Garden of Eden! When you are in a predictable structure—which is designed to get the maximum amount of people in the minimum amount of space—you aren't going to have much creativity. In existing facilities you are confined to an atmosphere that is created by what the people bring in with them as they enter the building.

There is a difference between designing the atmosphere of the heart and the atmosphere of the physical facility. The atmosphere of the heart is determined by the attitudes of the people who come to your meeting—their feelings, emotions and faith—all that is accessible to a newcomer. Our prayer is that the newcomer would experience a sense of coming home—of being truly wanted. There is a sense of expectancy of the arrival of God in our midst. There is a sense of the presence of God Who speaks with authority. There is an environment of joy, of genuine friendship, of grace—come as you are, and you'll be loved; come as you are, and you'll be changed; come as you are, and you'll never be the same. The intent is that the community expresses in tangible and intangible ways something that the newcomer would be hungry for in his soul.

When you are designing the physical environment, your job is to take every single element that the worshiper comes in contact with and to influence that thing as much as possible to have a positive impact on the meeting. Do I need to buy more chairs? Do I need to cover up the carpeting that looks old and worn out? Do we need better sound reinforcement? Any aspect of the environment that is in the physical realm is something that moves toward creating a milieu where it's easy to experience God. When we've succeeded, we have made the presence of God more accessible and understandable. And just maybe for the first time they can see that this God is real.

- Remember, everything is intentional from beginning to end—from before the first person arrives until the last person is long gone.

- Be intentional from the time the building is empty when you get there until the time the building is empty when you leave. The more that you can do intentionally—the more behaviors you can do intentionally rather than accidentally—the more things you can change to honor God. The more things that are working, the more you can understand why other things are or aren't working.

99 | Two words: sixty minutes.

No, not the TV show—we're talking about the move to a one-hour-long service. Get it all done in one hour or less. You may react to that thought with *Right. But you don't know our church culture or our community. We just can't get everything done in that amount of time.*

The motto In and out in about an hour has sold millions of pairs of glasses for LensCrafters for a reason. People in our culture live life in one-hour chunks of time. We have all been conditioned by the culture of TV to experience life in one-hour chunks of time. If our services don't fit into that time frame, we are bucking against the flow of life that is going on around us. This is the time frame that our TV-driven culture has trained 100 percent of us to think and emotionally and physically relate to, across all cultures in America.

There's no good reason for you to take more than an hour of your people's time on a Sunday morning for the service. We understand—some of the veterans will probably complain that they don't feel like they've had real church unless it lasts a certain length—sometimes that time is a lot longer than an hour. But if you hope to draw people into your church who will stay, you will need to adjust yourselves to them. They will not tolerate much more than an hour.

The make-up of the one-hour service looks something like this:

Worship	20-25 minutes
Transitions (including offering)	5 minutes
Message	30 minutes

The more newcomers you come in contact with, the more the 60-minute rule comes into effect.

This rule can be implemented within small groups, especially when small groups that take longer than an hour can get off track and become an end in themselves and a thorn in the side of a church planter.

Also, an hour limits the amount of content that you can present. That will allow you to focus on a specific issue. And that will allow you to focus the resources of your church on one thing.

Most Christians connect the length of time spent on a service with the spiritual value of that service.

Keep in mind that if you sell the 60-minute service to your team, you will need to abide by that or you will create numerous problems in your church systems. Many people who subscribe to the 60-minute theory go too long. They end up having people mad at them all over the church—especially in the parking lot.

If your people are looking for deep water instead of just a sip, then you need to have alternative meetings that last more than an hour. That is, you need to provide more choices that involve more intimacy and more involvement. We offer Big Wednesdays—nights when we have an extended worship time that lasts for 90 minutes. At the end of that time, we shift into a time of baptisms—sometimes baptizing as many as 75 people.

Most Christians connect the length of time spent on a service with the spiritual value of that service. But if you have newcomers—even if they are seeking strongly—we can assume they have an intimacy level of zero when they first walk in the door.

If God blesses you with more people, you're going to have to figure out how to take on the new people in the same amount of space. That means shorter meeting times. This means having spiritual depth in that time. Shorter services, doing more, going deeper—the blessing/curse of more people requires fitting more stuff into a certain amount of time.

These people have just one hour to offer—that's all they have to give you.

100 | Strategically look for your first couple of hires even before you are hired full-time.

Look constantly for quality staff. Consider your trips to conferences to be recruiting missions.

Consider this: Perhaps someone else will be brought on as paid staff even before you, because that hire might fit the strategic plan that God has for your church better than your coming on staff first. We've heard of that working out well in other church plants.

The ability to spot quality staff is a gift from the Lord. Ask Him for that gift. Receive it and you will have gotten something powerful from Him. Building a high-powered, quality staff is the key to growing your church past the first 200 to 300 people.

In one highly successful church plant that we are familiar with, the church planter hired someone else (a part-time prayer coordinator) before he himself came on staff, because he saw this hire as something strategic for the long-term growth of the church. He was apparently right in his hiring hunch. The church immediately prospered spiritually and numerically. They have gone on to plant a number of daughter churches as well.

What kind of people are you looking for?

- People who share your passion.
- People who exhibit a level of maturity that you would feel proud presenting to your people.
- People with a specific gift mix or skill set that is important right now to the life of the church (early on that gift mix will be music and perhaps technology).
- People with a clear calling from God. You know when you meet people if they have "it," and they know if they have "it" as well.
- People with a similar spiritual history that allows for shared values and priorities.
- People who are headed in the same direction spiritually and have the potential to become leaders as you reach out to your community.
- People who have bought into your vision for your church and for your community by giving strongly of their finances.
- People who have gifts you don't have and whose gifts complement your own.

101 | Allow God alone, not people, to direct your ministry priorities.

Don't get caught up in definitions of success imposed by others. The culture of the modern church sometimes causes us to get caught up in models that are not necessarily given to us from God.

Influence peddlers within your church have agendas—don't allow them to control the ministry path or focus.

Inside of yourself there are two sides of the same coin—fear of failure and ego. The ego side says, *I'm better than everyone else. This church is going to be a demonstration of how cool I am and my demonstration to other people.* This is a physical demonstration of arrogance.

The fear-of-failure side expresses itself by saying, *I'm not enough; I need to prove that I'm OK to my wife, to my peers and to the world.*

Those are the negatives.

Here are some positive goals we have found in other environments which have avoided those pitfalls. Guidelines which might look like:

- Is one person serving another person?
- Do you have an authentic, unforced community?
- Does it relate to the unchurched?
- Is it a natural fit for your people?
- Is it something you don't have to push very hard for your people to do?

Largeness is not the goal at any point. Some of the most successful versions of church have been the medium-sized churches we've had the privilege of interacting with over the years.

We believe in the power of the medium-sized church. I (Steve) have written a book that thoroughly examines the power of the church that runs between 300 to 500 people. It is titled *The Perfectly Imperfect Church*.

Goals that are self-defined will always cause you to land in frustration. You usually aren't wise enough to know what goals ought to look like.

102

**Show your kindness.
Get into the community!
Hang out with like-minded
church planters who can
relate to what you are going
through.**

Don't pay attention much to denominational imprimaturs.
There are many others around who are similar to you. You will
probably find more encouragement from people who are like
you—regardless of their denominational affiliation—because of
their church-planting connection. Over the years we have found
that church planters are more like us than any affinity possible.
That singular common bond transcends almost all theological
issues.

There is a need for tough-mindedness to be a successful
church planter. This sort of resolve is contagious.

- Find a fellowship of church planters, or start one.
- Attend church-planting workshops to build those relationships.
- Connect with church planters who are further down the
  road, can give you good feedback and can offer advice
  about where you currently are at in your planting
  process.
- New business owners are similar to church planters.
  Find ways of connecting with them and gleaning from
  them what they have picked up in their experiences.
- Your spouse needs to meet other church-planting
  spouses to understand more fully the burden of what's
  involved in the process and challenges of church
  planting.

103 | Get in the habit of church reproduction early, or you probably never will.

If you don't plant a new church within three years, you probably won't plant other churches.

One of the barometers of health in an organism is reproduction.

We encourage you to think about church planting from the very beginning. This may seem like a weird concept, but reproduction is the way of Mother Nature. It will allow you to be openhanded with your staff.

One of the barometers of health in an organism is reproduction.

It honors the fact that you will attract people with strong dreams and leadership capacities; it creates an atmosphere within the congregation that lets go—a launching, birthing environment. It forces your people to be openhanded.

If you miss the window of opportunity, it will be because of what we've seen happen—that people get caught up in the survival of their own church and become myopic. As a result, they lose a lot of what God has called them to as church planters. Church planting is a way of maintaining the edge. It's a way to stay connected to the world.

It brings about a level of confidence that says, *What we are doing here may not look dramatic yet, but the flow of what is happening here has created an environment from which leaders can go plant other churches.* And that helps you to feel that there's a backbone, a reality to what we are doing.

When some of your people go out to risk their lives in a church-planting endeavor, it is another barometer of knowing that you are up to something really good.

- Before your first public meeting, have a clear plan in place regarding your first church plant.
- Announce that this church is "born pregnant" with another church inside of itself and that you will be planting another church as soon as you reach an agreed-upon size. We recommend you plant by the time you have reached 300 weekend attendees. (That's assuming you will be sending off a group of 10 to 12 people to plant this new work—not a group of 50!)
- Begin to pray now for your first church plant.
- Start looking for your first church planter now.
- Start saving money for a start-up gift for your first church plant.

104 | Understand America's communication and visual media expectations.

If you get it right from the start, it will be such an advantage.

There is a significant front-end cost to having a high commitment to communication excellence.

If you look like you care, then you care. If you look like you are techies, then you are techies.

Outsource it. Technology literally is dominating. Lean into it, not away from it. There is sometimes a theological piece that says that we ought to lean away from technology. Paul used all of the technology that was available to him at the time.

Figure out what your thoughts and feelings on this are. Get help to see just what equipment you will need to enhance the type of service you are creating.

Technology should enhance worship rather than scream at someone sitting in your service.

Don't have technology just for the sake of technology. It should enhance worship rather than scream at someone sitting in your service.

105 | Realize how experiential people are becoming.

Having an experiential edge to your ministry is no longer an option—it's a necessity for modern worshipers.

People are getting used to using their five senses in experiencing God. You have to be aware of this.

What this generation requires is full participation in the giving of the gospel message. The reality is that people want to be engaged. Their level of exposure to quality media and their expectation of media of that nature are very high.

To touch and to see and to smell and to hear together make up an experience.

If you are new to this arena of information, start reading. Start listening to tapes. Go to Soularize.com or ooze.com. Start getting exposed to websites—smallfire.org, sacrimentis.com, freshworship.com and others.

This isn't to be the latest thing to do in the church because you got bored. This ought not to be the latest Christian craze.

Don't do it for a year and then be done with it. Learn from it, understand it. Grow in this area of understanding of what worship is and can be.

106 | Your ongoing means of communication will be e-mail.

Almost every student in junior high school has an e-mail address. If they don't have one, they can get a free one at hotmail.com or other sites.

Be awake and alive to the fact that we live in a digital world.

E-mail is timeless. I get it, and I get back to you when I get to it.

This is the preferred means of communication for most people now.

It's so great for a church environment. We wonder if God didn't design e-mail. Someone gives you his or her e-mail address. You now have access and can have entree into his or her life anytime you'd like. You can use it as a communication tool. You can use it as a sales tool. For example, if you are doing a series called "Intimacy with God," your members can forward your notes to a seeking friend. That outline can be sent around the world. We would give our e-mail address to any church in the world that would ask, but no one has asked us yet. We're still waiting for someone who is clever enough just to ask! The possibilities are vast.

Notes

1. Although we have done several hundred unique servant-evangelism projects over the past 16 years, there are a couple dozen that have been our bread and butter week in and week out.
2. Steve Sjogren, *Conspiracy of Kindness* (Ann Arbor, MI: Vine Books, 1993); Steve Sjogren, *101 Ways to Reach Your Community* (Colorado Springs, CO: NavPress, 2001); Steve Sjogren, *101 Ways to Reach Those in Need* (Colorado Springs, CO: NavPress, 2002).
3. James Collins, *Good to Great* (New York: HarperCollins, 2001), p. 21.

4. Aubrey Malphurs and Joel Aldrich, *Planting Growing Churches for the Twenty-First Century: A Comprehensive Guide for New Churches and Those Desiring Renewal* (Grand Rapids, MI: Baker Book House, 1998).

5. G. K. Chesterton, source unknown.

6. The *Passion* CDs can be obtained at www.worship.com.

7. See recommended reading list in appendix B.

ou can do anything else, do it. You're in charge of pennies, not doll
new church will have a unique way to do the tasks of ministry. Pe
e on; deal with it. Recognize that a very large percentage of the
h you gather will be already-converted people. What do you dr
ut? Is it a big church—or changed people? Lame facilities are OK.
. A lousy attitude isn't. Staff turnover is normal, not a sign of lurl
. Begin to delegate now. Have fun on the journey. Don't be n

RIGHT JOB DESCRIPTIONS

PHASE 1

0 TO 5 PEOPLE: MEET THE CITY

Senior leader role: Surveyor—What kind of place is this city?

Burning question: Are we going to make it?

Theme song: "We've Only Just Begun."

- Greatest asset: Attitude of *We have nothing to lose!*
- Greatest need: Just like in real estate—contacts, contacts, contacts.
- Growth strategy: Meet as many people as possible. Begin to tell your vision story to anyone who will listen—sane, insane or somewhere in the middle.

- Face of gathering: As many contacts as possible.
- Face of small groups: You have just one at this point, so it is all-inclusive, not focused in its makeup.

What I (Steve) wish I'd done differently at this stage: Prayed more, played more and fretted less.

5 TO 20 PEOPLE: MEET THE PEOPLE

Senior leader role: Gatherer.

Burning question: Where can I find people to talk to?

Theme song: "Heigh-ho, heigh-ho, it's off to work we go" (chant of the Seven Dwarfs).

- Greatest asset: An infectious smile and an enthusiastic handshake.
- Greatest need: Belief that you will succeed if you just keep at it in faithfulness. You will have plenty of moments of self-doubt and bewilderment about the vision you've stepped out to fulfill.
- Growth strategy: Gather others by yourself and with others who show up to help.
- Face of gathering: Begin concentrated servant-evangelism outreaches. You may have to do them by yourself, but this is a strategic time spiritually to begin these outreaches.
- Face of small groups: You lead the group(s) and begin looking for your first apprentices for future groups.

What I (Steve) wish I'd done differently at this stage: Taken the difficult individuals in groups less seriously. It doesn't take long until some EGR people show up. These are "extra grace required" folks.

20 TO 50 PEOPLE: GROUP REPRODUCTION

Senior leadership role: Philosopher (2 steps forward, 1.5 steps back).

Burning question: How many strange people can one city have?

Theme song: "It's Gonna Take a Lotta Love."

- Greatest asset: A great love for people.
- Greatest need: Belief that this venture is going to eventually succeed.
- Growth strategy: You are a seed planter, so plant lots of seeds of God's kindness and generosity around the city. Begin to really make a name for yourself. Your church will begin to become famous beyond your mere numbers by the actions that you are involved with if you concentrate your actions on servant evangelism and ministry to the needy.
- Face of gathering: Outreach projects in small-group subsets of about five people.
- Face of small groups: Leadership development with an eye to the future, to training apprentices.

What I (Steve) wish I'd done differently at this stage: Spent less time working on connecting with the scaffolding people and more time meeting a broad base of people in the community.

50 TO 120 PEOPLE: LEADERSHIP REPRODUCTION (HAVING BABIES)

Senior leader role: Plate spinner.

Burning question: What have I gotten myself into?

Theme song: "People, people who need people, are the luckiest people in the world."

- Greatest asset: Ability to multitask with relationships.
- Greatest need: Realism. Don't allow a bit of momentum to be taken too seriously. If you do, you will stop taking risks adequately, and your momentum will take a big step backwards.
- Growth strategy: Leadership development; more groups launched. Hold loosely onto leaders—you will go through two or three leaders to keep one at this phase.
- Face of gathering: Begin to hold churchwide outreach events.
- Face of small groups: Risk letting small groups take off. Experience failure along with success.
- Focus on small-group apprentices as the key to group multiplication. Begin closing down ineffective small groups—they need to know that it's OK to close, that ministries and groups are not permanent.

What I (Steve) wish I'd done differently at this stage: Worried less about what my denomination thought about my budding success.

120 TO 200 PEOPLE: GOING PUBLIC—BUILDING SYSTEMS

Senior leader role: Spokesman-salesman for your group.

Burning question: How can we help people find us?

Theme song: "Break on Through to the Other Side."

- Greatest asset: Your church's distinctiveness.
- Greatest need: To get through this stage, or size barrier, as quickly as possible and on to the 300 size.
- Growth strategy: Balancing out your outreach and your inreach activities. That is, having both excellent care for the poor and the lost through servant-evangelism actions (doubling up on your outreach is necessary) and, on the other hand, tightening up your gathering times—making your gathering times so excellent that you leave everyone always wanting more.
- Face of gathering: Reputation as servants in the community plus reputation for excellent gathering times.
- Face of small groups: Turbo groups for the rapid reproduction of small-group leaders.

What I (Steve) wish I'd done differently at this stage: Spent time refining my speaking skills—that is, invested in being helped by a speech coach.

PHASE 2

200 TO 300 PEOPLE: ORGANIZED CHAOS

Senior leader role: Trainer.

Burning question: What have I gotten these people into?

Theme song: "Helter Skelter."

- Greatest asset: Getting a clearer view of your preferred future.
- Greatest need: To be laid back in the face of all sorts of turmoil breaking loose.
- Growth strategy: Conveying your vision for this great new church in the city.
- Face of gathering: Extending the power and practice of serving out to the edges of your church—integrating serving into the very fiber of your church's being.
- Face of small groups: Haphazard experimentation—trying lots of things to find out what will work. Don't look for *the* way for doing small groups, but look for what works for you at this time.

What I (Steve) wish I'd done differently at this stage: Enjoyed the chaos instead of feeling like I had to gain control of it.

300 TO 500 PEOPLE: SYSTEM REPRODUCTION

Senior leader role: Human direction sign—no longer meeting people's needs, but directing them to where their needs can be met.

Burning question: Are we losing touch with people?

Theme song: "Goodbye Yellow Brick Road."

- Greatest asset: Multiple small groups.
- Greatest need: More small groups.
- Growth strategy: Activating the small groups into servant-evangelism teams going out to serve on a regular basis (i.e., every month).
- Face of gathering: Tweaking your weekend gathering times so they are more excellent. Getting the most out of your production elements at weekend celebrations.
- Face of small groups: Small-group matrix.

What I (Steve) wish I'd done differently at this stage: Worried less, enjoyed more. During this time it's easy to take yourself and your measure of success too seriously. Don't fall for that.

PHASE 3

500-PLUS PEOPLE: SYSTEM REFINEMENTS

Senior leader role: Visionary communicator.

Burning question: Are we going to make it?

Theme song: "It's Been a Hard Day's Night."

- Greatest asset: The testimony of what God has done through you.
- Greatest need: Hire gifted, like-minded pastoral staff who will release the people of your congregation to go into ministry.
- Growth strategy: You are growing by removing the obstacles to growth—that is, you are clearing the roadblocks that will keep you from going forward.
- Face of gathering: You will be gathering in multiple ways— through excellent weekend celebration times, through small groups and through massive servant-evangelism outreaches that are happening on a constant basis.
- Face of small groups: Small-group reproduction system in high gear.

What I (Steve) wish I'd done differently at this stage: Taken more seriously our role as a significant model church in the city.

ou can do anything else, do it. You're in charge of pennies, not dollars.
n new church will have a unique way to do the tasks of ministry. Peo
e on; deal with it. Recognize that a very large percentage of the
h you gather will be already-converted people. What do you dre
ut? Is it a big church—or changed people? Lame facilities are OK.
. A lousy attitude isn't. Staff turnover is normal, not a sign of lurk
. Begin to delegate now. Have fun on the journey. Don't be pi

GROWING PAST THE TEMPTATION TO QUIT

How to Not Leave the Ministry

BY STEVE SJOGREN

A wise veteran church man told me, "After living through 60 years of life, I am convinced that the most difficult job in the world is church planting." I agree. More than once I've told my wife, Janie, "There has to be a more lucrative way to be miserable." I've done a number of things for a living, and church planting has certainly proved to be the most difficult.

It's only natural that given the high level of stress in planting, there will be great turnover. I don't have scientific proof, but my guess is that the number one reason church plants don't succeed is because the senior leader quits. Several times in my first few years of planting, I actually did quit, at least for a day or two.

Remember that God is involved in your project and it's not just you by yourself sweating it out. Expect interventions from outside your situation. Once a man that I had never seen before, a retired farmer, came to me and said, "I don't know you, young man, but I feel you are to know that God has invested too much in you for you to quit now." He didn't know it, but my motivation had been at an all-time low. I had indeed been contemplating quitting my church plant. That word of encouragement from the mystery farmer has come back to me many times over the years as a source of encouragement.

Here are some wisdom points that I have walked in over the past years. I have found these to be golden principles as I have worked with church planters.

1. Tend your inner garden.

Amazing intensity can mount up in our hearts as we do the rugged work of church planting. Release that in the form of intercessory prayer. For me, this prayer isn't so much a grocery list of intercessory prayer, though I do keep a prayer list in my journal. I tell the Lord what He already knows. I bring to Him the specific issues that are pressing in on me.

You do have an inner garden. The only question is, What shape is it in? As the poem asks, "How does your garden grow?"

2. Pray deep prayers.

When Paul spoke of his groanings too deep for words—those inner prayers uttered by the Holy Spirit—I believe he was referring to the prayer he did to release the intensity that rested upon him.

3. Read Scripture.

For years I've told my church, "Five chapters a day keeps the pastor away." Without a routine, I would find it impossible to get my five chapters in a day. For the past few years, I've done more devotional listening to Scripture than I've read. I've purchased the Bible on audio CD and find it a very pleasant listen. Often I end up listening to more than my five chapters.

4. Write Scripture.

I've heard it said, "Girls keep a diary; boys write in their journals." Wordsmithing aside, during the past few years, I have been enriched in my times with God as I have done less reading of Scripture and more writing out of Scripture in my journal. It's simple. I write out complete verses, chapters and books of the Bible word-for-word into my journal. In the margin, I make comments on those verses that stand out to me. I have been asked, "Why write Scripture out? Isn't reading it good enough?" After 25 years of speed-reading, I have found it increasingly difficult to benefit from my time in Scripture. After all, some of those chapters have been covered as many as 150 times. What has been the result of my writing? I feel the love and appreciation that I once had for Scripture returning.

Also, I am slowing down. I tend to live and work at a pace of about 10,000 rpms. My friends and coworkers frequently comment on how much I get done with my skill at multitasking. There's nothing wrong with getting things done, but sometimes I can accomplish so much that I nearly do myself in. As I write my way through the Bible (I'm most of the way through the entire Bible at this writing), I slow down to the speed of my soul. It's at that speed that I hear God's voice, and I become aware of God's immediate presence and experience the renewal of the Holy Spirit.

5. Limit times with negative people.

Steer clear of those who bum you out. Be mindful of how much time you allow yourself to be exposed to negative people. In my experience, there needs to be a cap put on the amount of daily time we spend with people who bring us down. Once you've figured out who those negative folks are in your life, and you see them coming, start your watch. Give them a few minutes—maybe five at a stretch, maximum—and then make up an excuse for leaving their presence. You have far too much going on that requires a positive mental attitude to allow yourself to be brought down by these naysayers. That's literally what I do. I set my watch for the amount of time I allow myself to spend around these folks, and I abide by it. I make up about any excuse. I will pick up my pager and tell them I've been paged (that's partly true—I was paged a number of times that day already, and I just hadn't responded to them yet!).

6. Offer many light touches but few deep ones.
Don't spend too much time with just anyone. Move toward a mile-wide-and-an-inch-deep approach when it comes to counseling. No doubt this will seem like a superficial and limited treatment of some people's heavy-duty problems. Perhaps that is true, but for you to maintain your sanity in the first few years of planting, it may be a harsh fact of life that some of those who come to your church have needs that are beyond your ability to help. In many cases a kind word and a brief prayer is a sufficient and prudent response.

 Let's rejoice in each person the Holy Spirit sends us—in fact they are all gifts.

Each of the new churches I have planted has attracted a slew of chronically broken people like magnets. At one point I thought

I had a ministry to manic-depressives (those with bipolar disorder) because so many had found their way into our church. Let's rejoice in each person the Holy Spirit sends us—in fact they are all gifts. Make sure it is you—not the needy person—who defines the amount and type of care offered.

7. Live modestly.

Balance is an overused term. Clearly the physics of life require that one action brings about a reciprocating action. What goes up must come down. What gives out must be refilled.

Don't give in to manic living. Establish a routine of sanity. Find healthy ways to recover. Read the newspaper every day. Read normal magazines and books (not just on leadership and church growth!). Bicycle. If you can talk your wife into it, get a motorcycle.

At the end of some of my early days in Cincinnati, I would hear dozens of people a day say no thanks to my vision. I usually recovered by watching a decent flick. For me the movie wasn't the point. As much as anything, it was a matter of breaking the routine and clearing out the cobwebs of my mind. Remember, we are running a marathon, not a sprint.

8. Own what you can, but no more.

Enduring church planters know how to draw boundary lines. They can realize what is within their realm of responsibility and what is beyond their purview.

There are a myriad of out-of-control factors that enter into the picture when it comes to the establishment of a new church. Those factors change somewhat from day to day, but the church planter walks in the world of out-of-controlledness from day one of his church plant, and it seems there's no looking back from that time forth. That's just the way it is in the game of church planting.

9. Find friends.

James Taylor sings, "When you need a friend . . . I'll be there." A friend is someone who can be called upon at any time—day or night. No matter what your issue or need, they are available to listen and to lend support. This is someone you can call at 2:30 A.M.—and they will actually talk to you. Based on that definition, how many friends do you have?

If you are one who has many acquaintances but no friends, pray a couple of friends into your life.

Men tend to have many acquaintances but few, if any, authentic friends. Church planters tend to be unbalanced in life toward too much of a task emphasis and too little of a focus on relationships. Most planters have no one in particular they can turn to for support, encouragement and plain old fun.

If you are one who has many acquaintances but no friends, pray a couple of friends into your life. While you are at it, pray a couple more in for your wife as well. God's job is to provide friends for you. Your job is to pray and look and find them.

10. Quit an all-too-demanding side job.

If you are bivocational in the launching stage of your plant, don't forget why you are doing all of this—to launch a church! You did not move here to build a career in the secular workforce. If your job is robbing you of energy and enthusiasm beyond reason, find a new job. The ideal arrangement is a job that looks something like this:

- Pays an hourly rate.
- Has daytime hours so that your evenings are freed up to build leaders and launch small groups.
- Doesn't overly drain you emotionally or physically.
- Puts you in touch with a good cross section of your community.

I have found that jobs in sales or education tend to be all consuming and are therefore ill suited for planters.

11. Acknowledge leaders s-l-o-w-l-y.

It is common for leaders to trust volunteers too quickly in the early phases of a church plant only to discover that these were LWAs—leaders with an agenda. As church planters we are in a conundrum for several years in a new plant—we need leaders desperately, but most of those available to lead aren't leaders. Why is it common for these faux leaders to find their way to church plants? Those who have been rejected in the past by other churches find it attractive to start over at a new church where no one knows them. The challenge with leaders is this: to allow those who have failed in the past to get a fresh start, but at the same time to make leadership decisions that will allow the church to grow in the years to come. This is my conclusion on the issue: I must take into more serious consideration the larger work of God over the individual leadership choices. It's a goose and golden egg question. The golden eggs (individual leaders) are wonderful, but I must protect the goose (the local church) above all considerations.

12. Seek counseling.

Some will stumble on this point. But count on it—you need counseling. Planters lead spartan lives. They spend years being resisted, rejected, stressed out and sometimes even downright cursed. It seems unfair. We are just trying to bring Christ to people. We are lifelong Boy Scouts—trying our best to do our duty, seeking to do right. As the old joke goes, some little old ladies don't want to be helped across the street, no matter how loving we are. If we do have one of the most difficult jobs in the world, then an occasional counseling stint isn't unreasonable.

At several points in my life I have pursued prolonged counseling (i.e., several months of weekly meetings). Connecting with a skilled objective party has done wonders for me.

One note about choosing a counselor: As you seek help, I recommend you not limit your options to so-called Christian counselors. All things being equal, I would choose a Christian counselor over one who was not, but the quality of help varies greatly. I have wasted precious time with unskilled therapists. These days the health insurance industry is looking for the most bang for the buck. The less expensive, the better is their motto. The result—the competency level of counselors has dropped several notches over the past several years. Don't waste your limited time and insurance coverage with a soul helper who isn't much help, IXOYE on the card or not.

13. Celebrate success—even when it appears insignificant.

As a task-focused person, I find it easy to fixate on problems. Problems tend to expand to fill all the energy nearby. At those times it is almost impossible to see the great things happening around me. A way to avoid the frustration trap is to establish milestones in your planting journey. Keep track of and celebrate your 1st and 5th small group, for example. Rejoice in your 30th person and your 1st and 20th baptism.

14. Ignore invalid critics as much as possible.

An invalid critic is one who either speaks an exaggeration or an all-out untruth about your leadership. They might speak a word regarding people problems. At several points along the way in your first year, you will have some significant rejection issues to wrestle with. Someone will come, seem committed and then leave with an attitude. They will tell others who are still committed and in the group that you are not much of a leader, that you are not teaching the truth or that "this dumb little so-called church will never amount to anything" (a direct quote from one of my former members). If you are wired anything like me, on the heels of a conversation like that, you will be tempted to obsess on the critical words spoken. It isn't long until that situation can take up far too much of your mental energy. What's a planter to do? Here are a couple of policies I have developed in planting at Vineyard Community Church:

When someone leaves, have a consistent verbal response ready for all inquirers.

I've discovered that if you don't have a response for someone's departure, others will volunteer their own version of what happened. Sometimes their version is softer, but more often it is a harsher version of reality. If the person or family was visible in the fellowship, it is vital that you offer an explanation to those who ask. It helps me to write out key words in advance of giving a verbal explanation. "Yes, the Johnsons did leave recently. We're still friends. They were looking for a different kind of church—one that wasn't as outwardly focused as we are. That's just not who we are nor is it where we are going."

It is virtually always a mistake to make mention of the departure of a family to your entire group at a weekend celebration. To mention this is to revel in the disagreement of someone who didn't buy into the vision. I wouldn't mention the departure to anyone save the top couple of leaders, and even then I would state it in the most positive of terms—"They are pursuing a new ministry opportunity that is exciting. We bless them" (if you honestly can!).

Guaranteed—fewer people knew the person in question than you initially estimate in your shock of hearing that they are leaving. And of those who did know the person, few will think that it is a big deal that they left. In my years in Cincinnati with a large staff, only twice have we made mention of someone leaving, and they were highly visible staff. However, I am still approached five or six times a year with a request to mention someone's departure. I always say no.

Develop the Forrest Gump response skill.

That is, it's OK to smile, then ignore those who are trying to engage you in needless controversy. Every weekend I have one or more of those conversations with folks. I refuse to engage them in an argument. One friend of mine put it well: "It's hard to argue with an idiot." I've learned to shift into this mode temporarily. It has served me well.

When controversy strikes, set a time limit on how much you will talk about "it."

I tend to be a bit obsessive by nature, as are many church-planter types. When a significant problem hits that has the potential for some widespread emotional stirring, I find it challenging not to work on it until it is completely fixed. I like issues to be addressed and done with, and then I wipe my hands of the situation so I am free to move forward. The problem is, many challenges we face as pastors simply can't be resolved—at least in the short run. When your time limit is up for the day, refuse to talk about it any longer until tomorrow.

ou can do anything else, do it. You're in charge of pennies, not doll
new church will have a unique way to do the tasks of ministry. Pe
e on; deal with it. Recognize that a very large percentage of the
h you gather will be already-converted people. What do you dr
ut? Is it a big church—or changed people? Lame facilities are OK.
. A lousy attitude isn't. Staff turnover is normal, not a sign of lur
. Begin to delegate now. Have fun on the journey. Don't be of

PILGRIMAGE LANDSCAPES

BY MARK SCANDRETTE

Three years ago my wife, Lisa, our three kids and I moved from northern Minnesota to San Francisco to start a house-church movement among what we used to call urban postmodern peoples. We bought an old Victorian house in the Mission District—an eclectic, multicultural neighborhood, which included Latin American immigrants, old hippies, punk rockers, bohemian Marxists, art activists, young gay men, lesbians and dot-com hipsters. We chose San Francisco because of its long-standing reputation as the most progressive, postmodern and post-Christian city in America. This is where we wanted to work out faith and Christian community.

We had every hope that this venture would be successful. I had just finished a three-year stint working with students at a traditional church. They hated my best efforts at the classic youth ministry "thang"—the wanging electric guitar worship songs and comedy, à la hard-core gospel message, routine. There was a disconnect between the realities of their lives and the culturally shaped practices of our church. I had invited them to come to our house, "the shack," on Sunday nights. It started with Lisa, three students and me around a campfire in the woods behind our house. When more and more students started showing up with their nonbelieving friends, we moved inside. Our living room was packed with skate kids, punk rockers, hippie girls and sports and band people from seven different high schools. Everything we did was participatory and experiential. I led behind the scenes and mentored five or six senior high students who facilitated most of the meetings. We had lively discussions on pop culture, sexuality, death, philosophy and the Bible. We worshiped. We prayed. We celebrated Communion. We had ministry times where people would pray and speak prophetically over one another. The Holy Spirit manifested in some amazing ways! Students who had never been to a church were showing up with friends and engaging in our discussions, prayer and worship. They sensed a warm and different vibe. After six or eight months they would come to me and say, "Mark, what is this I hear about being saved?" We looked hard at the early chapters of the book of Acts and Paul's writings on the fellowship of believers—and gradually came to the realization that this ragamuffin crew of kids was fulfilling New Testament functions of a church.

Our very first experience leading a relationally based group happened five years earlier. Back then Lisa and I spent our time working with children and families in low-income housing projects. It grieved us to see that when these Jerry Springer-style families found faith, they didn't feel comfortable or accepted in our middle-class church. We also drooled over Acts 2:42-47, where the Church seemed like an empowered dynamic of relationships rather than a culturally bound institution. We wanted a simple and informal alternative to the highly organized form of the typical church. We invited two other couples to join us on Sunday nights to experiment with New Testament church life. Within two months there were 30 of us meeting, including 10 kids! It was a great mix of professionals, working class people *and* families from the projects. We ate meals together, met for worship and Communion and served one another in practical ways. It was a great experiment! But I was only 22 and was not prepared for the level of leadership and organization required to sustain such a group. So after a summer break, we didn't call the group back together. However, this experience gave us confidence that we could potentially catalyze a relationally based Christian community.

Roll forward to San Francisco 1998. In the first six months two house churches formed with 10 to 12 people per group. People were excited about the dream of true community and the possibility of seeing a faith movement happen in San Francisco, birthed from these house churches. But quickly things got weird.

Our group had a tendency to react to the traditional American expressions of the church. Many of us had never felt accepted by a church or had been hurt by church relationships. A lot of us were idealists who longed for the restoration of the church to that in the book of Acts and to its redemptive potential in society. And each of us faced some internal and external criticism for our decision to leave the dominant church paradigm. Let's face it: it takes a lot more commitment and participation to be in a house church than to be in an audience-based worship service. This led some of us to develop a rather dogmatic "biblical" rationale for the structure and functioning of our church. Since we were giving our lives to this and it was costing us so much time and energy, then it had better be the "right" way. We spent a lot of energy reinforcing and defending our position and "disciplining" those who weren't as ardent or committed to the model.

We were never able to settle issues of leadership and organization. All of us somewhat fit the sterotypical psychic profile of Generation X. Most of us grew up in single-parent households where we learned to distrust authority and to take care of ourselves. Others of us were reacting to overauthoritarian religious upbringings. Consequently, we feared and avoided anything resembling order, plans, organization or directive leadership. It had to be spontaneous and organic. There could be no leadership beyond the collective consensus. This made it extremely difficult for us to make decisions or take action.

Sometimes the people who most need a sense of Christian community are least equipped for community. We weren't prepared for the level of brokenness among the people in our church. Most of us wrestled with depression, addiction recovery, gender and sexuality issues, relational tensions or mental-disorder issues common to the population of San Francisco. We all made valiant efforts to seek God and to love one another. But as a group, we simply didn't have the collective energy to function consistently in a healthy way. In our immature or misguided efforts to love, we often hurt one another.

Our church stayed together for more than two years. There were some beautiful moments along the way: courageous acts of love and self-sacrifice, care for the poor and marginalized, generosity, shared living space, opportunities to witness, tender moments of affection and lots of memories—retreats, camping trips, hikes, long talks, hundreds of meals, etc. We did some things as a church that we hadn't seen or done before. We tried and did the best we could with the insight and resources we had.

One of the more painful disappointments was the unrealized dream of seeing our generation experience life with God. We sincerely thought that reforming the structure and functions of the church would unleash the power of the New Testament Church. In retrospect I believe our house-church ambitions were a premature solution to larger issues facing the people of God in the West.

We live in a society that is increasingly secular, post-Christian and postmodern—dramatically different from the cultural ethos and social structures that allowed for the expansion and maintenance of a Christian movement in the modern era (eighteenth through mid-twentieth centuries). This cultural shift has prompted many of us to deconstruct our modernist, conservative American evangelicalism. The modernist version of life with God simply doesn't work for us, in form or content. We thought that merely changing the form of the church would adequately address the challenges of an emerging postmodern era. But the deconstruction and eventual reconstruction must be more fundamental. I'm convinced that a proactive movement of faith will not come from this deconstructive phase or from a superficial reconstruction. Nor will it come from a preoccupation with maintaining "spiritual" market shares through pragmatic repackaging and image management of old-time modernist Christianity.

I did not avoid the temptation to use relationally based multiplication models as a utilitarian alternative to failing church-growth technologies. I wanted to be successful. We moved to San Francisco without adequate sensitivity to varying spiritual atmospheres. Our positive house-church experiences in the Midwest developed in a culture bathed in a Judeo-Christian ethos. As a pastor I had positional credibility, language and cultural fluency and an audience eager for what I had to offer. People were looking for the "*uber*spiritual" experience of a house church. We were naive to think that the same approach would be effective in a thoroughly post-Christian environment—with a population that was generally hostile to Christian faith.

In our quest for the recovery of transforming life, we hadn't gone far back enough. We were still coming up with answers that only work for people still in the shadow of a modernist Christian culture. We went to the book of Acts for a prescriptive solution, but the events there were prompted by a compelling primal reality—Jesus. We needed to go back to the Gospels and rediscover the goodness and beauty of the kingdom of God.

Jesus is the place where reconstruction begins. One time a guy in a tattoo shop told me, "Jesus is cool. It's just that the Church has [expletive deleted] with Jesus. I think Christianity was at its best when it was secret, hidden, and you could die for it." Jesus came announcing, "The kingdom of God is at hand" (Mark 1:15). His good news was that the creator is caring, present and now active, bringing all of life back into the Genesis vision—the world as God intended it to be. We have begun to embrace Jesus, not only as Savior, but also as teacher. Jesus is the way to life—and our way to life. He is the means and example for life in the kingdom of God.

In our exuberance to see a faith movement happen in our generation, we confused the questions. We started by asking, "What form(s) should the church take in this emerging culture?" We needed to be asking, "What does the life and teaching of Jesus mean in this time and place?" We made the church the Kingdom, instead of seeking the Kingdom as the people of God.

For now our family is exploring a primal pursuit of Jesus and His kingdom. We are acknowledging that we know a lot less than we thought we knew. We have a loose network of fellow postmodern pilgrim friends also working out life with God in San Francisco. Our gatherings are about practicing and imitating Jesus' life in our neighborhoods: eating with the homeless, creating art, engaging in classic spiritual disciplines, practicing hospitality, etc. Our vision has changed from a house-church movement to an indigenous Kingdom movement.

A while back we developed the following identity statement:

We are a movement of people in San Francisco, who, believing that our city is loved by God, seek a way of life that reverberates with the goodness and beauty of the kingdom of God.

Mark Scandrette lives with his family in the Mission District of San Francisco. He is cofounder of Re/IMAGINE!, an incubator for Kingdom living in San Francisco. He can be reached at Scandrette@aol.com.

ou can do anything else, do it. You're in charge of pennies, not doll
n new church will have a unique way to do the tasks of ministry. Peo
/e on; deal with it. Recognize that a very large percentage of the f
:h you gather will be already-converted people. What do you dr
ut? Is it a big church—or changed people? Lame facilities are OK.
. A lousy attitude isn't. Staff turnover is normal, not a sign of lurl
. Begin to delegate now. Have fun on the journey. Don't be pi

RECOMMENDED READING

Barna, George. *Grow Your Church From the Outside In: Understanding the Unchurched and How to Reach Them*. Ventura, CA: Regal Books, 2002.

Bennis, Warren, and Joan Goldsmith. *Learning to Lead: A Workbook on Becoming a Leader*. Cambridge, MA: Perseus Publishing, 1997.

Collins, Jim. *Good to Great*. New York: HarperCollins, 2001.

Collins, Jim, and Jerry I. Porras. *Built to Last*. New York: Harper-Business, 1997.

Cook, Jerry, and Stanley Baldwin. *Love, Acceptance and Forgiveness*. Ventura, CA: Regal Books, 1979.

Cordeiro, Wayne. *Doing Church As a Team*. Ventura, CA: Regal Books, 2001.

Donahue, Bill P. *Leading Life-Changing Small Groups*. Grand Rapids, MI: Zondervan, 1996.

Frazee, Randy, and Dallas Willard. *The Connecting Church*. Grand Rapids, MI: Zondervan, 2001.

George, Carl, Warren Bird, and Robert Coleman. *Nine Keys to Effective Small Group Leadership*. Mansfield, PA: Kingdom Publishing, 2001.

Gerber, Michael. *The E-Myth Revisited*. New York: HarperBusiness, 1995.

Goleman, Daniel, Annie McKee, and Richard E. Boyatzis. *Primal Leadership: Realizing the Power of Emotional Intelligence*. Boston, MA: Harvard Business School Press, 2002.

Kouzes, James M., Barry Z. Posner, and Tom Peters. *The Leadership Challenge*. San Francisco, CA: Jossey-Bass, 1996.

Mallory, Susan, and Brad Smith. *The Equipping Church Guidebook*. Grand Rapids, MI: Zondervan, 2001.

McLaren, Brian D. *More Ready Than You Realize*. Grand Rapids, MI: Zondervan, 2002.

Miller, Lawrence M. *Barbarians to Bureaucrats*. New York: Fawcett Books, 1990.

Moore, Ralph. *Starting a New Church*. Ventura, CA: Regal Books, 2002.

Needham, David. *Birthright*. Sisters, OR: Multnomah Press, 1999.

Sjogren, Steve. *The Perfectly Imperfect Church*. Loveland, CO: Group Publishing, 2002.

Welch, Jack. *Jack*. New York: Warner Books, 2001.

ou can do anything else, do it. You're in charge of pennies, not doll
n new church will have a unique way to do the tasks of ministry. Pe
ve on; deal with it. Recognize that a very large percentage of the
ch you gather will be already-converted people. What do you dr
ut? Is it a big church—or changed people? Lame facilities are OK
. A lousy attitude isn't. Staff turnover is normal, not a sign of lur
. Begin to delegate now. Have fun on the journey. Don't be pi

GLOSSARY

atmosphere architecting: Moving from simple planning of a church to dreaming and drafting a precise reality into existence based on the values and calling of the fellowship.

Big God: A strong awareness of the presence of the Holy Spirit in worship (whether that's music or holistic).

church: A group of 200 or more that gather together for worship. Technically, according to the biblical definition, where two or more are gathered there is a sense of a church, but for our purpose and in the context of modern culture, unless at least 200 are involved in the enterprise it isn't a long-term viable entity. Now we know this may anger you. Our point is that when a church reaches 200-plus people, it doesn't have to struggle continually for survival, and the group is large enough to self-gather.

church plant: A new group of hearty souls that feels called by God and is aspiring to the challenging work of building a church from scratch.

church planter: A courageous person who is convinced that he or she will be able to impact the forward progress of the kingdom of God by establishing a new church.

church planting: Simply the most effective means for expanding the Kingdom reign and rule of God upon Earth that is known to man.

critical mass: The size a budding congregation must grow to in order to self-gather rather than to rely strictly on the gathering ability of the senior leader. This number varies between 150 and 400, depending on a number of factors.

flavor: The specific filter through which a person views spiritual things. It has to do with his or her particular commitment to a style of ministry and worship, theological understanding and social expectations involved with being a disciple.

leader: A person who has a function in a church plant, but probably doesn't have a title or official office.

morphing: The ability to recreate oneself in order to become effective in the next chapter of one's leadership. This can also be true for institutions and groups. This can also be true for the way of doing things in a church.

outreach: The opposite of inreach. An action that focuses the love of Christ on someone a person doesn't know yet. It is taking the love of Jesus in many creative, practical ways to people outside those whom one normally associates with.

outward-focused church: A church that doesn't serve itself. Rather it serves the people who aren't attending yet. It serves with no hidden agenda. It serves freely with no expectation of receiving anything in return.

Phase 1: The "Will we *survive*?" stage. From 0 to 50 people.

Phase 2: The "Will we *grow*?" stage. Breaking the 200 barrier.

Phase 3: The "Will we *matter*?" stage. Growing past approximately 500 people.

the poor: That group of people consisting of the least, the lost, the left behind and the lonely, who are very close to Jesus' heart.

senior leader: A synonym for church planter. This is what a planter can be called after the initial plant is accomplished.

servant evangelism: A simple approach to sharing the good news of Jesus Christ that involves first approaching people with practical acts of kindness and profound generosity. This is the approach that we recommend one takes in connecting with the community when initially moving into a city. It is a profoundly effective way to get the attention of the people who are served because it helps people to see God in a way they haven't seen Him before. It is also a contagious activity in which the people in a church plant can participate.

turbo groups: Intense, short-running groups that are designed to raise up leaders in a short period of time—six to seven weeks. They are made up of hand-picked people who are likely to be able to start successful small groups at the conclusion of the training.

Web sites to check out!

www.servantevangelism.com

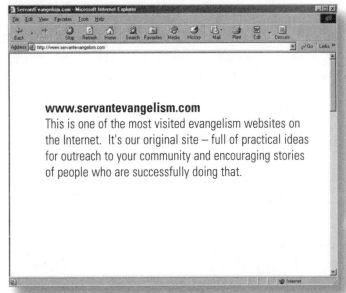

www.servantevangelism.com
This is one of the most visited evangelism websites on the Internet. It's our original site – full of practical ideas for outreach to your community and encouraging stories of people who are successfully doing that.

www.churchplanting.com

www.churchplanting.com
Come here for encouraging stories, demographic tools and connecting with other church planters from around the world.

www.topfive.org

www.topfive.org
This site is full of quick recommendations of products and services that church planters will find handy. Search our products, and make your own recommendations.

www.stevesjogren.com

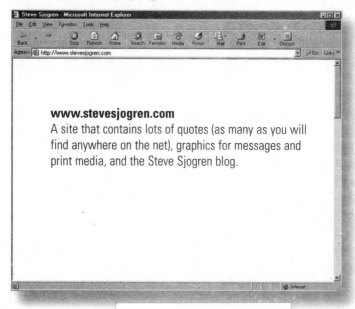

www.stevesjogren.com
A site that contains lots of quotes (as many as you will find anywhere on the net), graphics for messages and print media, and the Steve Sjogren blog.